THE SHEPHERD PSALM

REV. F. B. MEYER, B.A.

The
Shepherd
Psalm

≈

Rev. F. B. Meyer

≈

Keats Publishing
New Canaan
Connecticut

THE SHEPHERD PSALM

Shepherd Illustrated Classic edition published 1979

Library of Congress Catalog Card Number: 79-88308

ISBN: 0-87983-210-x

Printed in the United States of America

SHEPHERD ILLUSTRATED CLASSICS are published
by Keats Publishing, Inc.
36 Grove Street, New Canaan, Connecticut 06840

CONTENTS.

Illustrations

The lives of some men glow with the very life of God. They are incandescent with the inner flame of Christ's own gracious presence. They burn brilliantly with the Spirit from above. Such a man was F. B. Meyer.

Both his personal life and his prolific pen (he was the author of some seventy books) made an enormous impact upon his generation. To a lesser degree the legacy of his life in God has touched some of us in the latter half of this twentieth century.

I am one of those whose own experience has been enriched by reading several of his books. Along with authors like Henry Drummond, Oswald Chambers, Spurgeon, and Dr. Martyn Lloyd-Jones, his works have been used by the Gracious Spirit of God to lift the scales from my spiritual eyes; to see and grasp more clearly the enormous truths contained in God's Word; to come to know and love Christ more intimately.

During his own life F. B. Meyer was a minister in Great Britain with not only a burning compassion for the souls of his people, but also an equally great concern for their social betterment. The prostitutes and pimps were as much his concern as the dock workers on the waterfront, prize fighters in the ring, or the august members of Parliament.

He did much more than just preach and protest against the injustices of his day. He took positive steps to establish homes for unwed mothers, orphans, and other social outcasts.

F. B. Meyer had an enormous capacity for work. Blessed with a sturdy constitution, he travelled widely around the world, preaching, teaching and ministering tirelessly. Like

Sir Winston Churchill, he had the ability to catch a cat-nap almost anywhere, anytime. After a brief sleep he would awaken refreshed, able to carry on with remarkable energy and endurance.

He was a man of humble and contrite spirit, a true friend of God, with whom he kept close company. His favorite name for himself was "God's errand boy," very much in the same manner that Paul loved to call himself "a servant of Jesus Christ."

It had not been my privilege to read this book on the Twenty-third Psalm until just a few days ago (June 1979). As with so many of his observations, F. B. Meyer there discloses some insights into the Scriptures which could have come to him only from the Spirit of God.

Here I share several which impressed me at once:

"Unbelief puts circumstances between itself and Christ, so as not to see Him;

as the disciples did, through the mist, 'and they cried out for fear.' Faith puts Christ between itself and circumstances so that it cannot see them 'for the glory of that light.' Unbelief fixes its gaze on men, and things, and likelihood, and possibilities, and circumstances. Faith will not concern herself with these; she refuses to spend her time and waste her strength in considering them. Her eye is fixed steadfastly on her Lord, and she is persuaded that He is well able to supply all her need, and to carry her through all difficulties and straits."

". . . if you do not know which way to go, wait till you are sensible of the leadings of the Good Shepherd. Your life is wonderfully interesting to Him; every step of it is the subject of His thought. It will be a sore mistake and wrong for you to act without being sure of what He wishes you to do. And if you are not sure what that is, it is evident that the time has not yet come for you to move. Stay just where you you are. If you dare to wait you will be clearly shown your path, and the revelation will not come a moment too late."

He treats the Psalm from a profound and deeply doctrinal stance. Yet, as with so many of his writings, he proceeds to make a practical spiritual application that will ·enhance the life of any observant and obedient reader.

This little book, if read with an open and receptive spirit, will enrich the reader's life. Then he, too, like others of us, will give God thanks for this great, good man who went "home" fifty years ago.

Read, ruminate and rejoice in its green pastures.

W. Phillip Keller
Oliver, British Columbia
June 1979

PREFACE.

TO see a masterpiece of painting on the walls of an art gallery while a throng of conventional sightseers is pressing past is a very different matter to seeing it quietly on the walls of some stately mansion, when there is time to sit down and drink in the artist's thought, or catch the different lights of early morning, of noon, or of the fading day.

Perhaps the enjoyment is the more complete when some devoted lover of the work stands beside, telling the story of its daily effect upon his mind, and indicating subtle beauties which had escaped the first superficial gaze.

It is with some such intention that this book is sent forth — that, in the quiet of the sick-chamber or of the prayer-closet, attention may be again concentrated on this inimitable psalm; that the familiar words may be considered in the light of growing Christian experience; and that perchance some unnoticed beauty may be suggested by one who seldom comes to it without discerning some fresh reason to thank the Spirit of Inspiration that He ever led the sweet minstrel of Scripture to indite the Shepherd Psalm.

F. B. MEYER.

The Lord is my shepherd; I shall not want. He maketh me to lie down in green pastures: He leadeth me beside the still waters. He restoreth my soul: He leadeth me in the paths of righteousness for His name's sake. Yea, though I walk through the valley of the shadow of death, I will fear no evil: for Thou art with me; Thy rod and Thy staff they comfort me. Thou preparest a table before me in the presence of mine enemies; Thou anointest my head with oil; my cup runneth over. Surely goodness and mercy shall follow me all the days of my life; and I will dwell in the house of the Lord for ever.

THE SHEPHERD PSALM.

I.

THE PSALM OF PSALMS.

THIS psalm has sometimes been called the Psalm of the Crook. It lies between the Psalm of the Cross and the Psalm of the Crown. If the Twenty-second tells of the Good Shepherd, who died, and if the Twenty-fourth tells of the Chief Shepherd, who is coming again, the Twenty-third tells of the Great Shepherd, who keeps His flock with unerring sagacity and untiring devotion. No hireling is He. He asks no wage; He takes no reward. He counts not the cost. The sheep are His own. And in these sweet words we learn what He is towards them to-day, in all His shepherd tenderness and love.

Some have spoken of this psalm as a *creed.* I have it on good authority that one thinker at least, wearied with the perplexing questions that agitate so many hearts and brains in this strange questioning age, and pressed to give some positive affirmation of his creed, began reciting these words with solemn pathos of voice and kindling rapture of eye. And when he had finished the whole psalm he added : " That is my creed. I need, I desire no other. I learned it from my mother's lips. I have repeated it every morning when I awoke, for the last twenty years. Yet I do not half understand it ; I am only beginning now to spell out its infinite meaning, and death will come on me with the task unfinished. But, by the grace of Jesus, I will hold on by this psalm as my creed, and will strive to believe it, and to live it ; for I know that it will lead me to the cross, it will guide me to glory."

Yes, the testimony is true. And as one looking into some priceless gem may see fountains of colour welling upward from its depths, so, as we shall gaze into these verses, simple as childhood's rhymes, but deep as an archangel's anthem, we shall see in them the gospel in miniature, the grace of God reflected as the sun in a dewdrop, and things which eye hath not seen, nor ear heard, nor the heart of man conceived. Read into these words the meaning of the Gospels, and you have an unrivalled creed, to which all Christians may unhesitatingly assent.

Others have spoken of it as a *minstrel*. Before me lies a page that describes it in some such terms as these : that it is a pilgrim minstrel commissioned of God to travel up and down through the world, singing so sweet a strain that none who hear it can remember whatsoever sorrow has been rending and tearing at the heart! This, too, is true. This psalm speaks in language that the universal heart of man can comprehend. It exercises a spell that can charm away the griefs that bid a bold defiance to philosophy and mirth.

"It has remanded to their dungeon more felon thoughts, more black doubts, more thieving sorrows, than there are sands on the seashore. It has comforted the noble host of the poor. It has sung courage to the army of the disappointed. It has poured balm and consolation into the heart of the sick. It has visited the prisoner and broken his chains, and, like Peter's angel, has led him forth in imagination, and sung him back to his home again. It has made the dying Christian slave freer than his master, and consoled those whom, dying, he left behind mourning, not so much that he was gone as because they were left. Nor is its work done. It will go singing on through all the generations of time, and it will not fold its wings till the last pilgrim is safe and time ended ; then it shall fly back to the bosom of God, whence it issued, and sound on, mingled with all those harmonies of celestial joy which make heaven musical for ever."

But it may also be compared to *the holy of holies of old,* — the inner shrine of that splendid temple which rose, noiseless as some tall palm, at the bidding of Solomon. However eager or noisy might be the tide of human life that throbbed and surged through the narrow streets of the Holy City, or even pulsed in the temple courts, yet there was always one quiet and undisturbed enclosure where angel guardians stretched out their wings in calm repose over the ark of God. There at least was rest ; and if the priestly occupants had only been allowed to tarry in that secret place of the Most High, surely they had forgotten the fret and rush of life under the spell of that unutterable repose.

Dusty haste and restless anxiety must doff their garments and shoes ere they could enter there.

And all this is the psalm before us. It is an oasis in the desert; it is a bower on a hill of arduous climbing; it is a grotto in a scorching noon; it is a sequestered arbour for calm and heavenly meditation; it is one of the most holy places in the temple of Scripture. Come hither, weary ones, restless ones, heavy-laden ones; sit down in this cool and calm resort, while the music of its rhythm charms away the thoughts that break your peace. How safe and blessed are you to whom the Lord is Shepherd! Put down this volume and repeat again, in holy reverie, the well-known words to the end, and see if they do not build themselves into a refuge on which the storms may break in vain.

There is no question as to who wrote it, — David's autograph is on every verse. But

when and where did it first utter itself upon
the ear of man? Was it sung first amid the
hills of Bethlehem, as the sheep were grazing
over the wolds, dotting them like chalk-
stones? Or was it poured first upon the
ear of the moody king, whose furrowed brow
made so great a contrast to the fresh and
lovely face of the shepherd lad, who was
"withal of a beautiful countenance, and
goodly to look to?" It may have been.
But there is a strength, a maturity, a depth,
which are not wholly compatible with tender youth, and seem rather to betoken the
touch of the man who has learned good
by knowing evil, and who, amid the many
varied experiences of human life, has fully
tested the shepherd graces of the Lord of
whom he sings.

These words were surely first sung by one
who had suffered deeply; who had tasted
many a bitter cup; who had often been compelled to thread his way through many a

dangerous labyrinth, and beneath many an overhanging, low-browed rock.

We are told, in Persian story, of a vizier who dedicated one apartment in his palace to the memory of earlier days, ere royal caprice had lifted him from lowliness to honour. There, in a tiny room with bare floors, was the simple equipment of shepherd life, — the crook, the wallet, the coarse dress, the water-cruse; and there he spent a part of each day, remembering what he had been, as an antidote to those temptations which beset men in the dazzling light of royal or popular favour. So David the king did not forget David the shepherd boy. There was a chamber in his heart whither he was wont to retire to meditate and pray; and there it was that he composed this psalm, in which the mature experience of his manhood blends with the vivid memory of a boyhood spent among the sheep.

This only we say further, as we close this

meditation : that as this psalm hath virtue,
which streams to heal those who touch, so
it is true that its power lies in dwelling
so little upon man, and so much on God.
See how every verse tells us what *He* is
doing. This is the true policy of life. Unbelief puts circumstances between itself and
Christ, so as not to see Him ; as the disciples did, through the mist, " and they cried
out for fear." Faith puts Christ between
itself and circumstances, so that it cannot
see them " for the glory of that light."
Unbelief fixes its gaze on men, and things,
and likelihoods, and possibilities, and circumstances. Faith will not concern herself with
these ; she refuses to spend her time and
waste her strength in considering them. Her
eye is fixed steadfastly on her Lord, and she
is persuaded that He is well able to supply
all her need, and to carry her through all
difficulties and straits.

O trembling heart, look away, and look

up! Your sorrows have been multiplied indeed by looking at difficulties and second causes. Now cease from all this. Talk no more about the walled cities and giants, about the rugged paths and dark valleys, about lions and robbers; but think of the love, the might, and the wisdom of the Shepherd. Love that spared not its blood! Might that made the worlds! Wisdom that named the stars! Your salvation does not depend on what you are, but on what He is. For every look at self, take ten looks at Christ. Cease using the first pronoun, and substitute for it the third.

Tell us no more of your tears, your failures, or your sins; but tell us, oh, tell us, of the all-sufficiency of Jesus, and how your needs have been the foil of His deliverances. Sing again the old song of how all wants are swallowed up in the shepherd love of God. And emphasise each " HE " as you say again the psalm of childhood and of age.

II.

THE SHEPHERD LORD.

"The Lord is my Shepherd;
I shall not want."

THREE thousand years have passed away
since the sweet singer of Israel first
sang this psalm about the shepherd care
of God. Thirty centuries! It is a long
time. And in that vast abyss all the material relics of his life, however carefully
treasured, have mouldered into dust.

The harp, from the strings of which his
fingers swept celestial melody; the tattered
banner, which he was wont to uplift in the
name of the Lord; the well-worn book of
the law, which was his meditation day and
night; the huge sword, with which he slew

the giant; the palace chamber, from which his spirit passed away to join the harpers harping with their harps, — all these lie deep amid the debris of the ages.

But this psalm — though old as the time when Homer sang, or Solon gave his laws, and though trodden by the myriads of men in every succeeding age — is as fresh to-day as though it were just composed. Precious words! They are the first taught to our children, and perhaps the Holy Child Himself first learned to repeat them in the old Hebrew tongue beside his mother's knee in Nazareth; and they are among the last that we whisper in the ear of our beloved ones, standing in the twilight between the darkening day of earth and the breaking day of heaven. The sufferer in the sick-chamber; the martyr at the stake; the soldier on his sentry duty; the traveller amid many perils; the Covenanter; the Huguenot; the Vaudois, — these, and a multitude which no man can

number, have found in these words a lullaby
for fear, an inspiration to new life and hope.
"The Lord is my Shepherd; I shall not
want."

"THE LORD." It is printed in small capi-
tal letters, and wherever that is the case we
know that it stands for the mystic word
JEHOVAH. And so much in awe did the
Jews stand of that awful name that they
substituted for it some lesser word of God
wherever it occurred in their public reading
of sacred Scripture. Only once a year was
it pronounced, and that on the great day of
Atonement, by the high priest in the most
holy place.

Jehovah means the Living One, the self-
existent Being, the I AM; He who was, and
is, and is to come, who inhabiteth eternity,
who hath life in Himself. All other life, from
the aphid on the rose-leaf to the archangel
before the throne, is dependent and derived.

All others waste and change and grow old;
He only is unchangeably the same.   All
others are fires, which He supplies with fuel;
He alone is self-sustained.   This mighty
Being is our Shepherd.   Lift up your heart
to Him in lowly adoration, and say, "Give
ear, O Shepherd of Israel, Thou that leadest
Joseph like a flock; Thou that dwellest between the cherubim, shine forth."

But as we travel in thought down the ages
we meet a gentle, weary Man, on whom the
shadow of coming sorrow hangs darkly.   He
is speaking within a few miles of the spot
where these words had been first uttered
some twelve hundred years before.   Is it
treason?   Is it blasphemy?   Is it the rav-
ing of lunacy?   No; with all the marks of
self-possession and sober truth, He takes up
these very words, and applying them to Himself, He says, "I AM THE GOOD SHEPHERD."

Combine these two, — the august word for
the everlasting God, and the tender word

for the Saviour, — and we have a worthy title for our Lord, *Jehovah-Jesus*. Let us read it into our psalm, and say, with a new appreciation of its meaning, " Jehovah-Jesus is my Shepherd." What need can we have which may not be met by this twofold nature ? As Jehovah He has all power ; as Jesus all sympathy. As Jehovah He sustains all worlds ; as Jesus He ever liveth to make intercession. As Jehovah He is sovereign Lord of all ; as Jesus He still treads the pathways of this world by our side, whispering sweetly and softly in our ears, " Fear not, little flock."

" SHEPHERD." That precious word for God was uttered first by Jacob, — himself once a shepherd, — as he lay a-dying in his hieroglyphed chamber, and with the long thoughts of old age went back to the imagery of his early life, speaking of God as having " shepherded him all his life long." All through the Bible the golden thread runs, until in its closing pages we read of the Lamb who leads His flock to the river of water of life.

The Eastern shepherd occupied quite a unique position towards his flock, and a friendship sprang up between him and the dumb creatures of his care to which there is no counterpart among ourselves. Let us think ourselves into that relationship. In the early morning he would lead his flock from their fold to the pasture-lands. All day he must closely watch, lest harm should come to them from prowling beasts of prey or robber hordes. To the still waters he must lead them, that they may drink where no current shall frighten or endanger them, and at night he must conduct them back to the security of the fold. At a certain season of the year he must lead them yet farther afield, far away from his own home and the haunts of men, where he will live among them, scorched by the heat at

noon, and drenched by the dews at night. Should one of the lambs be unable to keep pace with the rest of the flock, he must carry it in his bosom. Should one of the flock go astray, he must search for it until he finds it, tracking it by the tufts of wool left in the briers and thorns. Should danger assail, he must be prepared to risk his life. Shepherds in the East look like warriors armed for fight, the gun slung over the shoulder, pistols at the belt, and club in hand.

Living on such terms, the shepherd and his flock are almost friends. They know him, and answer to their names. Some always follow close behind him, as his especial favourites, sure of his love. He can do almost as he wills with any of them, going freely in and out among them without exciting the slightest symptom of alarm.

Now all this is true of our Lord Jesus, that Great Shepherd of the sheep. He has a shepherd's *heart*, beating with pure and generous love that counted not His life-blood too dear a price to pay down as our ransom. He has a shepherd's *eye*, that takes in the whole flock, and misses not even the poor sheep wandering away on the mountains cold. He has a shepherd's *faithfulness*, which will never fail, nor forsake, nor leave us comfortless, nor flee when He seeth the wolf coming. He has a shepherd's *strength*, so that He is well able to deliver us from the jaw of the lion, or the paw of the bear. He has a shepherd's *tenderness*, — no lamb so tiny that He will not carry it; no saint so weak that He will not gently lead; no soul so faint that He will not give it rest. He pities as a father. He comforts as a mother. His gentleness makes great. He covers us with His feathers, soft and warm and downy; and under His wings do we trust.

Ah, He has done more! "All we like sheep have gone astray; we have turned every one to his own way." Punishment

and disaster were imminent ; but Jesus,
from His throne in eternity, saw the danger, and was filled with compassion for the
multitudes which were as sheep not having a shepherd. Therefore, because He
was the Shepherd, He offered to give His
own life as the substitute ; and God laid
on Him the iniquity of us all. Then was
heard the terrible summons, "Awake, O
sword, against my Shepherd, and against
the Man that is my fellow, saith the Lord
of hosts : smite the Shepherd." "He laid
down His life for the sheep," and thus
redeemed the flock by the blood of the everlasting covenant. Praise Him ! Praise Him !

"My." What a difference comes in
with that little word *my* ! "The child is
dead !" said one of the farm-servants, who
had carried the sick boy to his mother ;
"*My* child is dead !" said the mother.
"This estate is well known to me ; I have

trodden every mile of it from childhood,"
so speaks the gray-headed bailiff; "This
is *my* estate," thus speaks the heir.   So in
religion the difference between knowledge
and appropriation is simply infinite.   It
makes all the difference between being
saved or lost whether you say, "Jesus is a
Saviour," or "Jesus has saved me;"
whether you say, "The Lord is a Shepherd"
or "The Lord is *my* Shepherd; I shall not
want."   Even if, like Thomas, you could see
the Saviour in the clear light of reality, and
have every doubt removed, and His hands
offered to your touch, yet it would avail
you but little unless you could appropriate
Him by saying, "*My* Lord and *my* God."

Jesus waits to be appropriated.   He is
not content to be a Shepherd, a Good
Shepherd, the Shepherd of the holy
angels, the Shepherd and Bishop of count-
less redeemed ones.   His travail over you
will not be satisfied till you put your hand

on him and say, "*My* Shepherd." And
you may do that if you will. There is
nothing to hinder you. Do not tarry to
inquire if you are one of His sheep ; look
away from yourself to Him, and see if He
be not well qualified to be your Shepherd.
And the first cry of " MINE !" on your part
will be a certain indication that you are
included in that flock which He is leading
through many a tangled brake to the one
fold of heaven. "The Lord is *my* Shepherd ; I shall not want."

" I SHALL NOT WANT." Amid all the
sorrow and want of the world the Lord's
sheep are well supplied. The cry of
the worldling is contained in the weary
confession, "I perish with hunger." But
the boast of the saint rings through the
glad assurance, " My God shall supply
all your need according to His riches in
glory by Christ Jesus." His hired servants

have bread enough and to spare; how much more His own! "The young lions do lack, and suffer hunger: but they that seek the Lord shall not want any good thing."

Your experiences may seem to contradict that glad announcement; but perhaps you have not by faith sought and appropriated the supplies which have been placed ready to your hand; or you have not made your requests known unto God with prayer and supplication; or your hour of need has not yet fully come; or you have misunderstood your real need, and are asking for something which would do you harm. In one of these directions you must seek the reason of the apparent disparity between these glad, triumphant words and your own experience. For it is true for evermore that "there is no want to them that fear Him." He is able to make all grace abound, and He does make all grace abound. To Him be the glory for ever and ever.

Oh, bind this bright assurance to your heart; and whatever perils may menace and threaten you, whatever wants may assail, go forward, stepping out into the dark, encouraging your heart by this sweet refrain: "The Lord is my Shepherd; I shall not want."

III.

PASTURES OF TENDER GRASS AND WATERS
OF REST.

" He maketh me to lie down
In green pastures:
He leadeth me beside the still waters."

IN this sweet pastoral symphony, the first
verse gives the air, when it tells us that
there is no want to the man who lives under
the shepherd care of God. In the succeeding verses the harmony is worked out, and
the music in all its completeness is rendered
effectively.

The first want which, according to this
verse, he who belongs to Christ shall never
know, is the want of rest. This verse
breathes the very spirit of rest, as is even

more apparent in a more literal rendering of the words.   It may be rendered thus : "He maketh me to lie down in pastures of tender grass : He leadeth me beside the waters of rest."

What a delightful scene is thus conjured up before our fancy!   It is the scorching hour of an Eastern noon.   The air is stifling with fever-heat, and all the landscape is baking in the awful glare.   The very stones upon the hills burn the feet that touch them. At such a time woe be to the flock without a shepherd ; and to the shepherd who cannot find the blue shade of some great rock, the shelter of some bushy dell, or the rich and luscious pasturage of some lowland vale!

But there is no such failure here.   See where the pellucid stream is rolling its tide through the level plain.   Higher upward in its bed, when it was starting on its course, it foamed and fretted over its rocky channel, leaped from ledge to ledge, chafed against

its restraining banks, and dashed itself into a
mass of froth and foam. No sheep would
have drank of it then ; for the flocks will
never drink of turbid or ruffled streams.
But now it sweeps quietly onward, as if it
were asleep, — there is hardly a ripple on
its face ; every flower, and tree, and sedge,
as well as the overhanging banks, is clearly
mirrored on its surface, and every stone in
its bed may be clearly seen ; on its banks
the pasture is always green and luxuriant,
carpeted in spring by a thousand flowers ;
the very air is cooled by its refreshing presence, and the ear is charmed by the music of
its purling waters. No drought can come
where that river flows ; and the flocks, satisfied by browsing on the tender grass, lie
down satisfied and at rest.

WE ALL NEED REST. There must be
pauses and parentheses in all our lives. The
hand cannot ever be plying its toils. The

brain cannot always be elaborating trains of
thought.   The faculties and senses cannot
always be on the strain.   To work without
rest is like overwinding a watch ; the main-
spring snaps, and the machinery stands still.
There must be a pause frequently interposed
in life's busy rush wherein we can recuperate
exhausted nerves and lowered vitality.   There
is more permanence than many think in the
commandment which bids us rest one day in
seven.

But there is no part of our nature that
cries more urgently for rest than our spiritual life.   The spirit of man, like the dove,
cannot always be wandering with unresting
wing ; it must alight.   We cannot ever be
travelling up the rugged mountain pass of
difficulty, or traversing the burning marl of
discontent.   We must be able to lie down
in green pastures, or to pass gently along
the waters of rest.   There are three things
needed ere sheep or human spirits can rest.

I. *A consciousness of safety.* The growl
of a lion, the bark of a dog, the presence of
a little child, will be quite sufficient to spoil
the rest of a flock of sheep, and to drive
them trembling and timid into an affrighted
group. And how can we rest so long as we
feel ourselves liable to the attack of the roar-
ing lion of the pit? Who can rest so long as
eternal destinies lie uncertainly in the balance?

Against all this our Shepherd Jesus has
provided. He has Himself met the great
adversary of our souls, and has for ever
broken his power. We can never forget
that fearful conflict between the two, — the
malice of the one; the strong cryings and
tears, the anguish and bloody sweat, of the
other. It was not a time when we could
throw the balance of our weight into one
scale or the other; we were rather the prize
for which the battle was fought through the
long and weary hours. On the one hand
stood cruel hate and bloodthirsty destruc-

tion; on the other was mercy yearning to deliver, although at the cost of bitter agony and wounds, of which the scars shall remain for ever. In the end, the Good Shepherd gave His life for the sheep. No hireling coward He! His all was at stake. The flock was His own, given Him by his father; and He laid down His life for it.

But in that death He slew our enemy; as two antlered champions of the woods have sometimes been discovered side by side in death, because the one, in his own death-throes, had struck the other with a mortal wound. But God "brought again from the dead our Lord Jesus, that great Shepherd of the sheep, through the blood of the everlasting covenant." And now He lives to guarantee our safety. He has suffered all that there is to suffer. He has mastered all the opposition that there is to encounter. He has secured us everlasting deliverance from the slaughter-knife, from the demands of the divine law, and from the consequences of our own sins. "Who is He that condemneth? It is Christ that died, yea rather, that is risen again."

And now, O timid soul, be at rest! The blood-red brand which is upon thee is a sure token that thou art safe. He cannot have done so much for thee to lose thee now. In all moments of peril or dread softly murmur his name, *Jesus! Jesus!* and He will at once comfort thee by His presence and by His voice, which all the sheep know; and this shall be His assurance: "My sheep shall never perish, neither shall any man pluck them out of my hand."

"The Lord is thy Keeper." "We know that whosoever is begotten of God sinneth not; but He that was begotten of God keepeth him, and the evil one toucheth him not" (1 John v. 18, R. V.).

2. *Sufficiency of food.* A hungry sheep will not lie down. Main force will fail in

making it do so.   But the shepherd who can
provide it with plenty of good pasturage will
soon bring the most restless animal to lie
contentedly among the fragrant herbage,
while birds may settle on its woolly back
and bees murmur drowsily around.

We can never rest so long as the hunger
of the spirit is unappeased and its thirst un-
slaked.   Strange that men are so slow to
realise this !   Yet the whole drift of human
life seems impelled by the aching void within.
Conscious of their hunger, men try to satisfy
it with the husks that the swine eat ; but
they try in vain.   And there is no answer to
the unrest of the inward man until the voice
of Jesus is heard, saying, " He that cometh
to me shall never hunger ; and he that be-
lieveth on me shall never thirst."

Oh, to eat of the flesh of the Son of man,
and to drink His blood, — in hours of devout
reverie, in moments of rapt and intimate
communion !   This is life.   This is eternal

satisfaction.   Here are pasture-lands indeed,
and the rivers of His pleasures.

The Word of God may fitly be compared
to *green pastures*.   There is nourishment
there for all hungry hearts, — " enough and
to spare."   Nor do these pastures ever become barren or sear.   They are as green
and fresh to-day as when they were first
issued by the Holy Spirit.   Though multitudes of commentators have considered them,
and myriads of Christians have studied and
conned them, they cannot be pondered by a
loving and obedient heart without yielding
nutriment and strength.

There are many spiritual realities corre-
sponding to the *waters of rest*.   What is the
Lord's day but a water of rest ; or the hour
of worship ; or the long period of illness and
convalescence ; or the summer holiday ; or
the long halcyon period of spiritual prosperity, when it would almost seem as though
Satan had forgotten to tempt ?   At such

times it is sweet to know that He who anon
led to war or work is now leading to rest.

And in some cases, in the midst of life's
rush and pleasure, He beckons us aside to
rest with Him awhile, that we may have
leisure to eat.   He causes our hearts to
keep Sabbath and be at peace.   He makes
us drink of the brook by the way, and at
noon we rest with His flock in the blue
shade of the Rock in the weary land.

3. *Obedience to the Shepherd's lead.*   The
tenderest shepherd cannot bring a flock of
sheep to rest unless they follow him.   If
they lag far behind him, if they go astray
from him, if they take their own several
ways, then, however good the shepherd's intentions, they cannot but be thwarted and frus-
trated.   "My sheep," said Christ, "hear my
voice, and I know them, and they follow me."

This test of following the Shepherd's lead
is most important.   It is by no means wonderful that we lose our rest when we run

hither and thither, following the devices and desires of our own evil hearts. We substitute our plans for His. We insist on our schemes and stratagems. We crowd our days with much of our own, in addition to something of His. We do not look up often enough to see which way He is going and what He would have us to do. And so our rest is broken and lost. We must follow the Lamb whithersoever He goeth if we would be led to the living fountains of waters, which are fed from heavenly springs.

Oh, sigh not for the rest of God as if it were impossible for thee! The Good Shepherd waits to make thee lie down, and to give thee to drink long, deep draughts of rest. Only trust Him! Hand over to Him all that breaks the stillness of thy spirit, though it be but a gnat-sting ; and take from Him His own deep, sweet rest. Claim that He should make thee lie down by the arts of His gentle compulsion.

IV.

THESE words are among the most precious in this priceless psalm. They speak to the experience of many children of God, who are deeply conscious of the need of the restoring grace of the Good Shepherd. If He were alone to be followed, and if His influences upon us were always instantly and wholly obeyed, there would be no need of restoration. But we are not always susceptible and obedient to the heavenly leadings ; we easily relapse into states of lethargy and indifference, and it is necessary that we should be restored.

The most fruitful source of spiritual declension is the neglect of the Word of God and of private devotion. Just so long as the spirit of man keeps on terms of intimacy with the loving Spirit of God, while the Bible is regularly and prayerfully studied and the habit of retirement is maintained, there will be a regular growth in grace and in the knowledge and love of God.

If only the golden pipes are kept free and unclogged, there will be an uninterrupted flow of the golden oil to feed the flame of a holy life. We know all this. Our hearts have often tasted the sweet refreshing and holy encouragement which are found in these quiet, blessed hours spent in the most holy place. We know that there is nothing which is more productive of all that makes life worth having than communion with God. And yet this is the one exercise which we are most prone to hurry or neglect. The chapters of the Word of God are skimmed as a duty, as the surface of a mountain lake is touched

hefe and there by the breast of the wild-
fowl; while the morning or evening prayer
is uttered so coldly and perfunctorily that
it had almost have better been unsaid. Is
it, then, to be wondered at that the ener-
gies of the spiritual life decline, and sadly
need the interposition of some strong, wise
hand to restore?

Unconfessed sin is another cause of swift
spiritual decline. If there be a cause of
disagreement, however trivial, among friends,
they shrink from meeting; or if they meet,
there is a coldness and restraint which is
the more evident and painful in proportion
to the warmth and intimacy of their previous attachment. There can be no more
heart-union till the cause of estrangement
has been probed, and the wrong confessed
or the misunderstanding explained. And
the same principle obtains in the relationship
of the soul with God. When we sin, there
is generally a tendency to imitate Adam and

Eve in their concealment beneath the foliage of the garden. Before that sad yielding is the temptation of the devil. The happiest hour in all the day was that in which, as the evening breeze shed a delicious cool on the tropic heat, the voice of the Lord God was heard summoning them to commune with Him. But that sin makes the thought of fellowship unwelcome. Similarly we have learned again and again that unconfessed sin casts a dark shadow over our fellowship with God, and makes it irksome or perfunctory. Then we begin to exchange the open heart for the averted one, and put on the shy look and the formal phrase. And if the sin is not instantly confessed and put away, the little rift within the lute will widen, until it make the music mute.

Worldly society, with all its accessories, is another fruitful source of spiritual decline. It is impossible to spend much time amid the trifling talk, the inane conversation, the banter, the ridicule, the empty literature, the frivolous pursuits of what is called "society," without losing much of the fine edge, the holy temper of the soul. Man cannot touch a butterfly's wing without rubbing away some of the delicate down that covers it with microscopic feathers; and we are equally unable to be constantly living in the atmosphere of the salons of this world without sacrificing that indescribable delicacy and holiness of character which is God's choicest gift.

Of course, if the Lord Jesus sends us into the world to work for Him, He will keep us there. But we shall soon decline in spiritual health if we choose to live there; just as the country maiden will lose her bright, healthy colour, and show signs of consumption, if she always lives in the stifling atmosphere of the overcrowded room and amid the unwholesome conditions of our city life.

Neglect of some known command will also soon pull down the strongest spiritual health into the weakness of disease and decline. If only all the Christians who are now fencing with some known command of Christ would dare to obey it, there would be one of the greatest revivals that we have ever seen. You sometimes meet Christians who tell you that they used to be deeply " exercised " on certain matters.

What does the word " exercised " mean? Does it not mean that Christ was testing them by a certain definite command, and that they were, in point of fact, resisting Him, choosing their own way rather than His? And if this " exercise " of soul has stayed, what is the cause save this, — that the gracious Master has had the direct negative so clearly given Him, that it is of no further use for Him to ply the disobedient spirit, and so He has withdrawn from it? It may be saved, " so as by fire." But it can never know His tenderest love, or be used by Him for His loftiest ministry.

There are *many signs* of the declension of the soul: its restlessness; its spirit of captious complaining; its want of interest in the concerns of Christ's kingdom; its inability to testify for Christ or against sin; its unwillingness to admit that it is any different to what it used to be; its wincing beneath contact with the Word of God faithfully preached, and with the experience of others who are living in soul-health and in happy fellowship with God. Just as we have met with people afflicted with an insidious and dangerous disease who yet refuse to consider themselves so, and who fight against the desire of their friends to summon medical aid, so one phase of spiritual decline is the attempt to turn aside all suggestions of its presence, although gnawing the vitals of the heart. Then follows the sad admission, extorted as the years go on, that things are not as they were; which is followed by the hopeless conclusion that they cannot now be mended.

How welcome it is to turn to *the restoring grace of the Saviour!* Nature is full of great restorative processes. Directly a rent is made in her hillsides, she begins to festoon it with grasses, ferns, and creepers. When a wound is caused in our flesh, and the red blood breaks through the broken rampart as it passes, it begins to build up the breach, so that presently soundness takes the place of the lacerated aperture. Even when a rent is caused in our families by the death of some dear invalid, whose presence had given a new thoughtfulness to all the inmates, and whose death makes a breach almost irreparable to the survivors, then time with its healing influences begins to repair the yawning void.

So, spiritually, the blessed Spirit of God is ever brooding over human hearts to do His choice and beloved work of reparation and restoration. When the sheep is missing from the flock, He goes after the truant until He finds it, and restores it to its place among the rest. When one piece is missing from the completed circle of His crown, one jewel from His breastplate, He rests not till it is replaced. When one child is away in a far country, His own joy is at an end till he is back.

O gentle, tender-hearted, pitiful Saviour, how eager Thou art in pursuing these, Thy chosen ministries to Thy weak and unworthy children!

Christ uses *many restorative ministries.* Sometimes it is the word of a friend or minister. Or it may be a hymn breathing the fragrance of a holy heart and speaking of a happier past. Or it may be a paragraph, a sentence, in some biography or religious treatise. Not unfrequently it happens in this wise: you are away in the country, walking solitarily and moodily, when there is a burst of sunbeams, or of song-notes from the brake; or, without any natural cause, you are suddenly aware of the gentle, thawing, all-pervasive influence of the grace of God, which touches the deepest springs of the heart, and softens it, and leads it to contrition and prayer. Is not this experience something like that resulting from the look which Jesus cast at Peter, and which sent him out to weep bitterly, and was the first stage in his restoration?

Let those who want to understand the whole philosophy of restoration read the marvellous story of the way in which the Good Shepherd restored the soul of His erring apostle. We can only enumerate the stages here. He prayed for him, and warned him. From the midst of the rough crew that did their will on Him, "He turned, and looked upon Peter," — not angrily, nor harshly, but with the tenderest reproach. He gave a

special message to the angels that they
should bid the women summon Peter amid
the rest on the resurrection morning, show-
ing how constantly he had been in the
Saviour's heart all through His sorrows.
He met him alone on the world's first
Easter day, and permitted him to pour
out the story of his sorrow unrestrained
by the presence of any besides themselves.
He gave him an opportunity of thrice attest-
ing his love, to wipe out the memory of the
thrice denial. And this is not more than
He will do for any of us.

Oh, do not wait for days or weeks to
elapse, ere you apply to Him for His restoring grace; but just as you are, dare to trust
Him to do it now. While the throb of passion is still beating high, and the deed of
shame is recent, look up to Him, and claim
forgiveness first, and in the same breath ask
Him to put you back immediately in the very
place which you occupied before you fell.

And then, though as yet no answering joy thrills your heart, you will be able to exclaim, in the assurance of faith, " He restoreth my soul."

Yes, and for those who dare to claim it there is another promise still more reassuring, which tells us that " He will restore the years that the canker-worm has eaten," — giving back to us opportunities and privileges which we may seem to have forfeited for ever.

V.

THE SHEPHERD'S LEADING.

"He leadeth me in the path of righteousness
For His name's sake."

"HE leadeth me." What a wondrous link between those two personal pronouns! The chasm between the Shepherd in glory and His poor sheep might seem to be an infinite one; but it is bridged by this one sweet, tender word, "leadeth." As in the East the shepherd always precedes the flock, to discover the greenest patches of grass, and the least stony path, so does Jesus ever keep in front of the soul that trusts and loves Him. And it is our part to allow as small a space as possible to intervene between His footsteps and our own.

We must be willing to be led. There is so much natural impetuosity in us to shoot on in front and "prospect" for ourselves. Is that not so? And out of this restlessness there arises so much of the fret, and chafe, and disappointment of life. We think we can do so much better for ourselves than Christ can do for us. We doubt whether there is not something outside the limit of His will which it might be worth our while to snatch at. We are inclined to run before, or linger behind, or go off to forage on the right and left. We take a long time ere we learn that the place of usefulness and blessedness is in following the lead of Jesus. We are much more liable to imitate some scheme which our judgment may have passed after a hurried hearing of its claims than to ask where Christ wants us to be, and whither He is leading.

The one ambition of our being should be to be sure that we are resolutely following the Shepherd whithersoever He goeth; according to His own assurance, when He putteth forth His own sheep, "He goeth before them, and the sheep follow Him."

These words make a considerable demand upon our faith. Of old, the apostles could see Him in front of them as He went up to Jerusalem, and they followed Him in fear. But that is impossible now. We cannot see that gracious form treading earth's dreary pathways, and casting its shadow upon the sands of time. We love Him whom we have not seen. We follow Him whom we cannot behold. But though He be viewless as the air, or as the attraction by which the sun conducts the worlds through space, yet His leadings are distinctly discernible by the trusting, loving heart.

We detect His leadings in many ways. In the drift of His example and in the direction of His advice contained in the Gospels; in the counsel of a friend, the message of a sermon, the monition of a text flashed into our memories; as well as in those inner promptings of His Spirit which come we know not whence, and bear us we know not whither. Sometimes the way opens up before us quite marvellously where it had seemed closed; as when a vessel, threading her way through a labyrinth of rock, finds a space of shining water beckoning it from the jaws of reef which threatened it. At other times a strange impulse seizes us, which, after due thought and prayer, we are constrained to follow.

This only we would insist upon: if you do not know which way to go, wait till you are sensible of the leadings of the Good Shepherd. Your life is wonderfully interesting to Him; every step of it is the subject of His thought. It will be a sore mistake and wrong for you to act without being sure of what He wishes you to do. And if you are not sure what that is, it is evident that the time has not yet come for you to move. Stay just where you are. If you dare to wait you will be clearly shown your path, and the revelation will not come a moment too late.

Oh, do not say that you are so stupid that you can never know His will. You always were dull of apprehension, and your very nervousness to understand aright has sometimes made you too flurried clearly to apprehend the simplest directions. But obtuseness of the intellect matters little to Christ. He can deal with that, and He will. If He cannot make you understand in one way, He will in another. It is the business of the Shepherd to lead the willing sheep aright. The only thing which obstructs His guidance is the obtuseness of the heart and will; we are frequently too self-willed or too impetuous to await His time.

In the previous verse the psalmist declared that the Shepherd led beside still waters; and the inference might have been that when the feet were cut or the muscles strained by the clamber up the rocky mountain track, or that when the course lay amid deep, damp glens overshadowed by heavy forests and overhanging rocks, — that at such times the sheep was following its own wild way, outside the tender guidance of its Lord. And so the psalmist takes up the metaphor again, and tells us that there are other walks by which the Shepherd is leading us to our home. Not always beside the gentle streamlet flow, but sometimes by the foaming torrent. Not always over the delicate grass, but sometimes up the stony mountain track. Not always in the sunshine, but sometimes through the valley of the shadow of death. But whichever way it is, it is the right way, and it is the way home.

Christ's leadings are always along "paths of righteousness." And what are these but right paths ? They are not only consistent with the divine rectitude, but they are justified by the review of the spirit, when in after-days, looking back on them from the eminence to which they have led, it confesses that they were *right paths*.

You hesitate at this. You say that you cannot feel that God's ways with you have been right. You are puzzled by their mystery. You are almost driven to despair by their mazy difficulties, their inexorable demands. Such feelings are not to be marvelled at as you sob them out in the ear of God. And He is very pitiful; "for He knoweth our frame; He remembereth that we are dust."

Only do not judge God's ways while they are in progress. Wait till the plan is complete. Wait till the tapestry is finished, and you can see the other side where the pattern will be worked out. Wait till the silver-paper is torn off the worsted-work and the blending of the colours is disclosed. Wait till you have got out of the vale to the mountain brow. Wait till, in the light of eternity, God can call you aside and reveal to you His purposes.

Meanwhile, trust ! " All his paths drop fatness." " All the paths of the Lord are mercy and truth." If it is true that " His path is in the mighty waters," it is also true that He leads " by a right way to the city of habitation." Let us not judge God by an incomplete or unfinished scheme ; let us have patience till the end shall justify the path by which we came. In the breaking dawn of eternity we shall discover that God could not have brought us by another route which would have been as expeditious or as safe as the one by which we have come. Would that we had the faith to look up from every trying circumstance, from every fretting worry, from every annoyance and temptation, into the face of our Guide, and say, " It is the right way, Thou great Shepherd of the sheep ; lead Thou me on ! "

" Lead Thou me on,
O'er moor and fen, o'er crag and torrent, till
The night is gone."

But we do not need to plead with Him
for this. He is pledged to do it for the
sake of His own great name. " He leadeth
me in the paths of righteousness *for His
name's sake*." Remember how eager Moses
was for the honour of the name of God.
From many a saintly lip have the words
broken, " What wilt Thou do for Thy great
name ? " The name denotes the honour
and character of God. These are impli-
cated ; these are at stake ; the right leading
of the saint is guaranteed by their immuta-
bility.

What is His name ? " Wonderful ? " Then
there is a claim on the marvellous working
of His power to overrule everything to our
highest good. " Counsellor ? " Then there
is a claim upon His unerring wisdom to work
out a scheme which will fill heaven with ad-

miration. "The mighty God?" Then there is a claim on Him to do nothing inconsistent with divine integrity and glory. "The everlasting Father?" Then there is a claim on Him to deal no less tenderly than a father with his child. "The Prince of Peace?" Then there is a claim on Him in accordance with the sweetness and loveliness of His heart, the memories of His cross, and the tenderness of His benediction of peace.

"For His name's sake." What a plea that, to look right up from the heart of man to the heart of Christ, sure that He will not deny Himself, or belie His character, or do aught inconsistent with His tender love to those for whom He died!

Tell us Thy name, O wondrous Shepherd, going on before, and leading us by way of Gethsemane and Calvary to the garden of the Easter morn, and the sward of the ascension mount! And as we catch Thine answer, melodious with love, we will trust and not

be afraid ; we will follow thee whithersoever
Thou goest ; and we believe that we shall
find that no step of the path was inconsistent with the leadings of a Love wise and
strong and tender as the heart of God.

VI.

THE VALLEY OF SHADOW.

" Yea, though I walk through the valley
Of the shadow of death,
I will fear no evil; for Thou art with me."

IN all Scripture there is no verse more familiar than this. No Bible figure has made a more lasting or indelible impression. This picture of the close of our lives, with a dark valley at the end of their sunny pathway, was hung up long ago in the halls of memory, as we first learned to lisp these venerable words; and though much has happened since then, it holds its place, and will while memory endures. In millions of cases these have been the last words uttered by dying saints; and it is in the highest degree

probable that they will be gently uttered by many of those who read these words, as the spirit passes the borderland into "its ain countrie;" unless the Lord come first, and we miss the passage of the valley, being caught up to meet Him in the air.

Methinks I see that valley now. The Shepherd is conducting His flock towards their fold in luxuriant pastures, and in quiet resting-places. But suddenly the path turns downward, and begins to wind towards the ravine below. On the one side is a precipice, yawning in sheer descent to the steep river-bed, where the water foams and roars, torn by jagged rocks. On the other side the mountain-firs cast a sombre shadow in the deepening twilight. The path still plunges downward, until it passes into a deep and narrow gorge, overhung by the frowning battlements of rock, which almost touch overhead; while the trees join hands, bough enclasping bough. It would be dark there in the most brilliant noon. To linger there after sundown would be to court the ague. All along its course are the lairs and haunts of ravenous beasts. Such is the valley of the shadow of death, through which the Great Shepherd once went alone, and by which He now conducts all His flock to their home. The foremost ranks have long ago emerged into the sunshine; others are now passing through its dark shadows; and ere long we, too, may be beneath them.

This figure gives us some comforting thoughts about death. It is not a state, an enduring condition, or an abiding-place. It is a passage, a transition, a valley through which we walk. The valley may be darksome and lonely, and infested with evil things; but we do not pitch our tent there; we pass through it to our rest. In death the spirit leaves the body and passes out, just as an artisan will leave the work-

shop at the evening hour, shutting blinds
and doors as he passes out to his home,
and leaves it deserted and still; but his
voice is to be heard in his home circle, as
he makes glad the wistful hearts that had
waited for him, and whose joy had been
incomplete till he came.

In Damascus there is a long, dark, narrow lane, ending in a tunnel. It has been
there for ages. The traveller descends and
passes through; but on the other side he
emerges into the courtyard of an Oriental
palace, flashing with colour and sunlight.
This is a figure of a believer's death.
Christ is called the first-born from the dead.
Dying is being born out of the confine-
ment and darkness of earth into the glorious
light and liberty of the heavenly life. It is
a physical act which affects the body, but
does not touch the faculties or acquirements
of the individual soul. "Absent from the
body, present with the Lord." No staying

in a state of unconsciousness ; but an exodus, a passage, a walking through a brief
valley, sunshine on this side, sunshine on
that, and just a moment, a parenthesis, a
hand-breadth of gloom.

Death is the gate to life.   Our beloved
are not dead ; they are the living, who
have passed through death into the presence of the King.   And whensoever we
stand beside our dear ones, called to this
exodus, of which the Apostle Peter speaks,[1]
we may address them with words of comfort and of hope : " Go forth, O Christian
soul, from this world, in the name of God
Almighty, who created thee ; in the name
of Jesus Christ, the Son of the living God,
who suffered for thee ; in the name of the
Holy Ghost, who was poured out for thee ! "

Yet the valley is dark.   The pain of the
body often depresses the spirit and over-

[1] 2 Peter i. 15 (*exodus*).   The word occurs in one
other instance in the New Testament (Luke ix. 31).

casts it with a gloom, which is often erroneously attributed to spiritual causes. It is hard to part without sadness from those who have been the beloved fellow pilgrims of the march. There is, moreover, a sense of loneliness; for though it is peopled with pilgrims, — three thousand each hour,— yet each goes alone. *"Je mourrai seul."* Nor are elements of darkness wanting through the machinations of our direst foe, who delights in the moment of mortal weakness to accumulate objects of dread before our failing sight.

At the best it is a solemn thing to die. The hardened desperado may meet his end without a shudder. "There are no bands in his death : his strength is firm." But in proportion to the nurture of the spirit in all refined and tender feeling it is impossible to quit the receding shore, and make for the sea, darkling under the clouds of night, without a sense of seriousness and sobriety.

The befitting pace is aptly described as a walk : " Yea, though I *walk*."

But at the worst, death is only a shadow. It is "the valley of the shadow of death." Christ met the substance, we encounter but the shadow. The monster is deprived of teeth and claws. Our Theseus has destroyed him who had the power of death, that is, the devil ; and has delivered them who through fear of death were all their lifetime subject to bondage. He has abolished death. And we who belong to Him may boldly cry, " O death, where is thy sting?" Ah, the wasp stung the Good Shepherd to death, and has left his sting fixed in that cross where He died.

A shadow is the exact counterpart of its substance. But it is not in itself harmful. The shadow of a dog cannot bite; of a giant cannot kill ; of death cannot destroy. The prophet says that death is a veil cast over the face of all nations; but a veil is harmless enough. Besides, you cannot have a shadow unless there be a bright light shining somewhere. The shadow is temporary, the light eternal ; for " God is light, and in Him is no darkness at all."

But this imagery may stand for other experiences besides dying. We have often to pass through dark valleys on our way home. The road to the heavenly Jerusalem lies through the valleys of Baca, where eyes wax red with weeping, and tears brim into pools. The great dreamer, in his description of the Pilgrim's Progress, places the passage of the valley of the shadow in the middle of his course. Between the House Beautiful and Vanity Fair there lies such a description of *this* valley as could only have been written by one who had passed through its ravines.

" Now morning being come, he looked back, not out of any desire to return, but to see, by the light of the day, what hazards he had gone through in the dark. So he saw more perfectly the ditch that was on the one hand, and the quag that was on the other; also how narrow the way was which lay betwixt them both; also now he saw the hobgoblins and satyrs and dragons of the pit, but all afar off (for after the break of day they came not nigh); yet they were discovered to him, according to that which is written: 'He discovereth deep things out of darkness, and bringeth out to light the shadow of death.'"

We pass through many a valley of shadow ere we reach THE *valley.* And whenever we feel our souls overcast we should stay to consider if there be a cause arising from our neglect or sin. If there be, a moment's confession will bring us out again into the light. But if there be none, so far as we can tell, then let us be brave to plod on. Every step has been measured out for us, even as it has been trodden before us. And God is testing us to see whether we can trust Him in the dark as well as in the light, and whether we can be as true to Him when all pleasurable emotions have faded off our hearts as when we walked with Him in the light.

There is a good purpose in all these shadowed valleys. They test the quality of the soul. They reveal our weak places. They unveil the stars that peer down through the interspaces of rock and tree. They make us follow the Shepherd closely, lest we lose Him. They teach us to value, as never before, the rod and staff. Blessed are those that do not see, but who yet believe; and who are content to be stripped of all joy and comfort and ecstasy, if it be the Shepherd's will, so long as there is left to them the sound of His voice, and the knowledge that He is near.

Listen to the courageous declaration of the saintly soul, boasting of its fearlessness: "I will fear no evil." There is no fear in love. Perfect love casteth out fear. Nothing else can do it. You may argue against fear. You may deride it. You may try and shame it. But all will be in vain. If you would master it you must expel it by the trust which is born of love. A man comes home faint and famished, his nature craves for food; but as he enters into his house he learns that his child, suddenly stricken with fever, is lying at the point of death; and in a moment he has forgotten his hunger in the paroxysm of love and grief with which he bends over the tiny feverish form, and hastens to moisten the dry lips. Thus the lower passions are subdued in the soul by the higher. And so it happens that the most timid spirit which is conscious of the presence of the Good Shepherd can sing as it passes onward through the gloom, and its notes vibrate with the buoyancy of a courage which cannot flinch or falter. "Yea, though I walk through the valley of the shadow of death, I will fear no evil." "God is our refuge and strength, a very present help in trouble. Therefore will not we fear."

It is very well to say, "What time I am afraid, I will trust in thee;" but it is still better to say, "I will trust, and not be afraid."

Sorrow and dying make Christ's presence real. Have you ever noticed the change in the pronoun? Hitherto the psalmist has spoken of the Lord in the *third* person; but now, as he moves down into the dark, he draws closer to the divine Leader and Guide, speaking to Him in a whisper, and saying *Thou*. In the green pastures it was enough to speak of "He;" but now there is need for the closer, tender address. When things are going well with us we may content ourselves with talking about the Lord; but when the sky darkens we hasten to deal with Him and talk to Him directly. The child which had been playing about the room will run to your knee and cling closely to your bosom as soon as the thunder-clouds gather, and the wind moans through the

house.   In this way death-chambers become
presence-chambers.

The darkness is sometimes too dense for
us to be able to see Christ.   But faith can
always be sure that He is there ; not because
of the evidence of sense or feeling, but because He has said, " I will never leave thee,
nor forsake thee."   He cannot break His
word.   He has not left us alone.   He is
looking down on us with unabated tenderness.   The depths may sever Him from the
apprehension of our love ; but neither death
nor life, nor height nor depth, can separate
us from the strong grasp of His faithful and
unchanging affection.   Yea, "the mountains
may depart, and the hills be removed ; but
His kindness will not depart from thee,
neither will the covenant of His peace be
removed."

"The darkness and the light are both
alike to Thee," O Christ, who didst tread
the dense darkness of Gethsemane and Cal-

vary, — alone, desolate, and forsaken of Thy
Father.   But Thou knowest the way, since
Thou has trodden it.   Thou art as near to
us as when we can see and feel Thee near.
And Thou wast lonely that we might never
be lonely ; Thou wast forsaken that we might
never be forsaken ; Thou didst tread the
wine-press alone that each poor timid child
of Thine in all future ages might be able to
sing the words of undying comfort : " I will
fear no evil : for Thou art with me."

VII.

COMFORT THROUGH THE ROD AND STAFF.

"Thy rod and Thy staff they comfort me."

WHATEVER the valley of the shadow
of death may stand for in our Christian experience, there is no doubt that the
lonely spirit, in its passage through it, stands
in urgent need of comfort. From the beginning to the end of Scripture there is no refrain more frequent or more consolatory than
the thought embodied in the words, "Comfort ye, comfort ye, my people, saith your
God." Indeed, it would almost appear as
if the eternal God had set to Himself the
task of comforting His people as a mother
comforteth her first-born.

All true comfort emanates from God, through the work of the Holy Spirit. whose comfort is especially mentioned in Acts ix. 31 ; and any who would experience God's comfort in all its tender helpfulness, let them read perpetually in the Word of God, that through patience and comfort of the Scriptures they may have hope (Rom. xv. 4).

It would sometimes appear, indeed, that God puts us into special circumstances of difficulty and trial, in order that He may make manifest to us the infinite resources of His consolation ; just as we need to go out into the dark night in order to behold the stars. But the great point brought out in these words is that the Almighty God, our Shepherd, comforts us by His rod and His staff. How is it that these two badges of the Shepherd's office, which seem rather to speak of discipline, can possibly bring comfort to tried believers ? It is this point which

we desire for a moment to elucidate; and
may we not hope that the God of all comfort will reveal to us fresh sources of comfort,
that we may be able to comfort others with
the comfort wherewith we ourselves have
been comforted of God?

What is the Shepherd's rod? It is surely
the symbol of His defending power. It is
the sceptre which He carries as the supreme
Shepherd-King. It is the weapon by which
He strikes down our adversaries, even though
it be heavy with chastisement for ourselves.
In passing through some rocky fastness or
shadowed valley where wild beasts have their
lair, and hill-robbers hide in many a darkened
cave, a shepherd needs to be well armed with
heavy club or ponderous rod, that he may
deal death-giving blows to lion, or bear, or
stealthy thief imperilling the safety of one
of his charge. And does not this suggest
the protecting grace of Christ our Lord, who
is ever on the alert to ward off from us

threatening ills, whether they emanate from the prince of the power of the air, or from those malicious human foes to whose presence in this life our psalmist so often alludes, and who have their counterpart more or less in the lives of us all?

Many who may read these words spend all their lives under the shadow of a great fear. They dread the outset of temptation, before which they feel themselves as impotent as the withered leaves of autumn before the gusty gale; they fear that one day they will become the prey of the lion, or fall into the hands of a Saul. Would that they might transfer the responsibility of keeping their souls into the hands of their faithful Redeemer, confident that He will be about their path, and their lying down, so that they may "dwell safely in the wilderness, and sleep in the woods." The Breaker goes before the flock, smiting down all opposition with irresistible might; and God Himself is at the rearward of the flock, defending it from all attack from behind.

O timid hearts, dreading every spiritual and temporal evil, — like children going down a dark lane, in dread lest at every turn they should meet some terrible ogre or object of dread ; startled by the sigh of every breeze, and by the whitened bole of every hollow tree, — would that you could realise how absolutely Christ assumes the care of all who trust Him! The one question is whether you have so completely handed over the responsibility of your lives to Him as to make Him the sole custodian and safeguard of your being, both for this world and the next. From the defending rod or club of the Great Shepherd we may derive abundant comfort ; because it is written, " My sheep shall never perish, neither shall any [man or devil] pluck them out of my hand."

What is the staff ? We would rather call it the shepherd's crook, which is often bent or hooked at one end. It is associated as inseparably with the shepherd as the goad is with the ploughman. Beneath it the sheep pass one by one to be numbered or told. By it the shepherd restrains them from wandering, or hooks them out of holes into which they may fall ; by it, also, he corrects them when they are disobedient. In each of these thoughts there is comfort for the tried children of God.

We are numbered among God's sheep as we pass one by one beneath the touch of the Shepherd's crook. Our names may be unknown among the great and learned, but they are written in heaven. Our dwelling-places may be lowly and ungarnished among the mansions and palaces of the rich, but we have "houses not made with hands, eternal in the heavens." Our sphere of ministry may be limited, and our work in the trenches, preparing for the foundations, far away from the shoutings with which the topstone is placed upon a finished pile in the sunny air; but we shine as stars of the first magnitude in the sight of God. We are accounted as the small dust in the balance, as smoking flax or bruised reeds; but in the eye of our Heavenly Father we are prized as very precious jewels, entered in His inventory, and destined to shine in the regalia of His Son before the gaze of all worlds.

Words were spoken once among the exiles in Babylon which we may fitly apply to ourselves in this connection. Gathering at night by the waters of Babylon, they hanged their harps upon the pliant branches of the willows, as they swept in the current of the stream beneath, and they wept as they remembered the ruins of their beloved Jerusalem. Then in their midst the prophet voice was heard bidding them lift up their eyes on high, and behold the starry hosts; also they were reminded that God called all these by names by the greatness of His might; and then followed the magnificent apostrophe: "Why sayest thou, O Jacob, and speakest, O Israel, my way is hid from the Lord, and my judgment is passed over from my God?" And to each weary heart treading the dark valley of sorrow I would speak comfort in the selfsame words.

The myriad stars of heaven seem to make up one huge flock. Their Shepherd is God, who is driving them through space; or who watches them, as it were, resting on the heavenly slopes as a flock of sheep on the downs at night. And He has a name for each of them. Is it therefore to be supposed that He will not be as minute in His care of each one of us? Will He not have a name for each of us? Will He not number us when he tells the tale of His sheep, even as He numbers the hairs of our heads? This very morn He touched you with His staff and counted you. You are the destined object of His care. Is it likely, then, that

He will suffer you to perish, or want any good thing?

By the Shepherd's staff we are also extricated from circumstances of peril and disaster into which we may have fallen through our own folly and sin. When Peter through his unbelief began to sink in the waves, the Saviour caught him and supported him, so that they walked together to the boat. And this is only a sample case of our Shepherd's tender care; for very often sin not only grieves Him, but it plunges us into circumstances of misery and trouble which threaten to overwhelm us.

At such times He is not unmindful of His own; and though we may seem to have forfeited all claim to His care, yet He is "a very present help in time of trouble;" He does not permit us to reap as we have sown. He averts the full penalty of our own mistakes and misdeeds. He comes after us in the wilderness, not staying His foot until He has discovered the pit into which we have fallen, from which He does not fail to drag us forth; placing us on His shoulders if we are too weak to walk, and bringing us back; satisfied with no other recompense than that we are safe. "Thus saith the Lord God; Behold, I, even I, will both search my sheep, and seek them out. As a shepherd seeketh out his flock in the day that he is among his sheep that are scattered; so will I seek out my sheep, and will deliver them out of all places where they have been scattered in the cloudy and dark day." Oh, the long-suffering patience of Christ, who will not permit us to be overwhelmed by the sorrows and penalties which we may have incurred, but will reach out His crook to drag us back from the death that we had courted!

By the staff the shepherd also corrects His sheep. At first there seems but little comfort here. It is not pleasant to any one of us to be corrected. The smart stroke of the staff is painful. Yet there is consolation in the reflection that God must care for us, or He would not think it worth His while to expend time and thought upon our chastisement. Who troubles to take to the lapidary's wheel common flints and stones of the beach? The stone that is deeply cut, the diamond which is carefully polished, the metal which is plied with intense heat for weeks and even months, must have proved themselves to be of excellent worth. What gardener would spend time and pains over a tree which, after repeated trial, had refused to bear fruit? Is it not the bough which has already borne luxuriant clusters that receives the incessant attention of the husbandman? "Whom the Lord loveth He chasteneth, and scourgeth every son whom He receiveth. If ye endure chastening,

God dealeth with you as with sons."
Welcome, then, O children of God, each
stroke of the Shepherd's staff! Get comfort out of every smart by the thought:
" My Shepherd must love me tenderly, or
He would never treat me thus; and then
turn the heart towards Him in eager desire
to know the lesson He would teach, and to
miss nothing of the benefits which He in-
tends.

So we journey slowly through the valley,
learning many a lesson of comfort which
we hide in our hearts. We are almost content to suffer because of the rich revenue
of blessing which accrues. With us, as
with the oyster, every wound becomes the
origin of a pearl. And there is this also:
that our own experiences make us very
tender towards the failures and sorrows of
others, and we are able to join in the glad
outburst of the apostle who said, " Blessed
be God, even the Father of our Lord

Jesus Christ, the Father of mercies, and the God of all comfort; who comforteth us in all our tribulation, that we may be able to comfort them which are in any trouble, by the comfort wherewith we ourselves are comforted of God. For as the sufferings of Christ abound in us, so our consolation also aboundeth by Christ."

VIII.

THE BANQUET.

" Thou preparest a table before me
In the presence of mine enemies."

AT first it seems difficult to catch the exact sequence of the psalmist's thought, as he turns from the sheep-cotes to the festal board. And yet the demands of the spiritual life so far transcend all earthly analogies as to demand that more than one metaphor should be employed, one supplying what the other lacks, so that the true conception of our relationship to God may be complete.

Now it is of course very helpful to think of oneself as a sheep, and of Christ as a Shepherd ; but there can be no

93

fellowship between the dumb animals and their watchful keeper. The little child that comes from the shepherd's shealing to meet its father has more intimate fellowship with him, though it can hardly articulate its words, than the dumb creatures of his care.

The psalmist, therefore, seems to say, "I am more than Jehovah's sheep; I am Jehovah's guest." It is a mark of great intimacy to sit with a man at his table; in the East it is essentially so. It is not only a means of satisfying hunger, but of intimate and affectionate love. Hence the aggravation of the psalmist's sorrow, as he said, "He that breaketh bread with me is he that lifteth up his heel against me." Nor was it possible for our Lord to give any more touching proof of His love for His wayward follower than to dip a sop, and pass it to his hands. Here, then, arises before us a rich theme for meditation while we compare life to a seat at

God's banquet-table, eating the things which
He has prepared.

We sit at the table of God's daily providence.
Our Heavenly Father has a great family.
He is weighted with the concerns of a uni-
verse. All sentient things depend upon His
sustaining power. Not a seraph cleaves the
air but what derives his power of obedience
from his sovereign Lord ; and not a mote of
life floats in the sunbeam, flashing in the
light, but it is dependent upon the light and
life of the central Sun, before whom angels
veil their faces.

And yet, amid all the infinite variety of
nature which God is supplying constantly,
He is surely most attentive to the needs of
those who, in an especial sense, call Him
"Our Father." We are His pensioners ;
nay, better, — we are His children ! All
the stores of His divine provision must fail
before He can suffer us to want. He may
sometimes keep us waiting until His hour

has struck; but just as He will never be one moment too soon, so He will not be a moment too late. He will cause a widow woman to sustain us with the barrel of meal, which, however often scraped, will yield a fresh supply. He will rain bread from heaven, so that man may eat angels' food. He will multiply the slender store of the boy's wallet, so that present need may be met, and stores accumulated for the future.

On a recent Sunday evening, a sick member of a congregation, debarred from attending her customary place of worship, entrusted to the hand of the minister a two-shilling piece, which he was to hand to a poor widow known to them both. It so happened that he encountered her slowly making her way to the church, and at once handed to her the coin. But he was hardly prepared for the immediate response: "I did not think that He would have sent it so soon." On further inquiry he discovered that she had placed her last coin that day in the collection, and was entirely dependent upon such answer as her Heavenly Father might send to her trustful prayer that He would provide for her next meal. Evidently she had been accustomed to close dealings with God, and had learned that His deliverance is timed to arrive "when the morning breaks," — the morning of direst need ; the hour when pride and self-sufficiency have expired, but when faith and hope stand expectant at the portals of the soul, looking for the deliverance which cannot be long delayed.

I never shall forget the story of an old man discovered sitting in one of the seats of York Minster, within a short period of closing time, and who had been sitting there since the early morning, waiting. He had come to the city to find his daughter ; but, having missed her, had found himself without friends or food, and with his last coin spent. Not knowing whither to turn, he had found his way into the splendid minster, and had sat there the livelong day; because, as he said, he thought the likeliest place to find his Father's table was in his Father's house. Need I add that his need was fully satisfied?

God's children seem to think that they are no better off than men of the world. And, according to their faith, so it is done unto them. If we do not exercise faith and claim God's provisions, ought we to be surprised when we do not receive them? If, on the other hand, we would dare to put our finger upon His promises, which bind Him to meet His children's need, though the young lions lack, and suffer hunger, we should find that our God would be equal to all our emergencies, and that not one good thing would fail of all His promises. When men indicate certain cases in which God's children have pined to death, it is always wise to inquire whether they were living in believing fellowship with Him, and whether they had claimed the fulfilment of His specific pledges. It is very unbecoming, to say the least, that God's children should be as fretful about their daily bread, supposing they are using all lawful methods to obtain it, as the children of men. Was it not with a tone of reproach that our Lord said, " After all these things do the Gentiles seek ? " What could be more assuring than His own words, backed by the experience of His own life, — " Your Heavenly Father knoweth that ye have need of all these things ? "

What would you say if, when school-time came to-morrow morning, your little boy, before he started with unwilling feet to school, entered your larder and busied himself in examining its contents, with especial reference to your provision for dinner? Would he not legitimately incur your displeasure ? Would you not say, " Be off to school, and leave me to care while you are gone?" Would you not rebuke him for his want of simple trust? Oh, that we might learn lessons from our babes, and believe that life is one long residence in one of the mansions of our Father's home; and that the time can never come when the table is quite bare, and when there is nothing for our need! He may suffer you to hunger, because there are some devils which will only go forth by prayer and fasting; but, sooner or later, His angel will touch you, saying, "Arise and eat;" and on the desert floor you will find, spread by angel hands, a banquet, though it be nothing more than a cruse of water at your head, and cakes baked on the hot stones of the wilderness, for your repast.

God also prepares the table of spiritual re-freshment. Can we ever forget that episode — among the most charming incidents in the forty days — in which, as the weary

fishers emerged with empty boats from a
long, toilsome night, they found a banquet
spread for them, by the tender thoughtfulness of their Lord, upon the strand of the
lake? As soon as they touched land they
saw a fire of coals, and fish laid thereon, and
bread. And is not this an emblem of our
Lord's perpetual treatment of His children?
Tired, disappointed with fruitless toils, agi-
tated by conflicting hopes and fears, we
often pull to the shore trodden by His
blessed feet; nor do we ever approach Him
without finding that He has anticipated our
spiritual requirements, and that "His flesh is
meat indeed, and His blood drink indeed."

Writing to the Corinthian Christians, the
Apostle Paul said that, inasmuch as Christ
had been slain as our Passover Lamb, we
must imitate the children of Israel, who,
with closed doors and girded loins and san-
dalled feet, stood around the table eating of
the flesh of the lamb, whose blood on the

exterior of their houses demanded their deliverance. "Christ our Passover is sacrificed
for us : therefore let us keep the feast."
The life of the Church between the first and
second advents is symbolised by the feast
on that memorable night. With joy in our
voices and triumph in our mien, we stand
around the table where Christ's flesh is the
nourishment of all true hearts, straining our
ear for the first clarion notes which will tell
that the time of our exodus has come.
Christian people are very much too thought-
less of the necessity of feeding off God's
table for the nourishment of spiritual life.
There is plenty of work being done ; much
attendance at conferences and special mis-
sions ; diligent reading of religious books ;
but there is a great and fatal lack of the
holy meditation upon the person, the words,
and the work of the Lord Jesus Christ.

Will each reader of these lines stay here
for a moment, and ask if he knows anything

of the interior life of meditation which is ever deriving fresh sustenance from a consideration of the Lord?

It was only the other day that I was rebuked by the habit of a well-known Roman Catholic bishop of whom it is said: "The first point of his rule was early rising, which he faithfully practised to the last day of his life, and often recommended to others. He was the first on foot at his palace, and began his prayers and meditation between four and five o'clock in the morning, and never spent less at them than an hour. He often did this with his memoranda in his hand, so as to recall past graces, and thus rekindle the flame. Nor did it seem as if any hour passed in his crowded and stirring life without by some direct act refreshing his soul by communion with God."

And, in addition to this daily practice, he set apart one or two weeks in every year that he might quietly meditate more patiently

upon the great mysteries of redemption.
This is what he said : "One must, by constant meditation on the great mysteries of
incarnation and the redemption, plunge oneself more and more in the love of God, which
is the greatest grace of one's life. I will
occupy myself more and more with our Lord,
with His earthly and divine life, with His
hidden, suffering, and glorious life. May my
own be hidden in God in Jesus Christ ! "

*We may especially apply these words also
to the table of the Lord's Supper.* This is
emphatically a table which God has prepared ; which not only perpetuates the memory of the night in which our Lord was
betrayed, but which enables us to raise our
wandering thoughts, and to fix them on Him
where He is now seated. There is no mystic
change made in the bread or in the wine.
The bread remains bread, and the wine wine,
to the end of the simple feast ; and yet, at
the moment of partaking of these elements,

the pious heart does realise that, by its faith and holy thought, a distinct blessing is communicated to its invigoration and comfort. It is well, of course, at that solemn moment, to recall the agony and bloody sweat, the cross and passion, the precious death and burial; but it is equally incumbent to look through the azure depths and to follow the Master through their parted folds, so as to feed upon His resurrection life, and to participate in the perpetual Eastertide of His existence.

It is very helpful, where possible, to communicate at least once a week, that we may clearly learn to lift all life to the level of the Lord's table, to be at every meal as at a sacrament, and to use all the emblems of nature as means of holy fellowship with Him. How can we enough thank God that in this sense also He has prepared a table before us?

There is much comfort in the three words "prepared for me," because it would seem to

indicate the *anticipatory care of God.* He
does not allow us to be taken by surprise.
He does not let his children ask for anything
the need of which He has not foreseen.
Just as He has prepared beforehand the
good works in which we are to walk, so has
He prepared beforehand the food by which
His workers shall be nourished. All our
life's path is lined by cairns beneath which
our Forerunner has placed the victuals which
we shall require. "Thou preventest me
with the blessings of Thy goodness." The
table is spread before the hunger comes.
The spring is bubbling in the shade before
mother and child sink fainting on the sand.
The angel of the Lord's host has not only
taken possession of the hostile country, but
has provided of the old corn of the land.
God provisions His castles before they are
besieged. "Thou *preparest* a table before
me."

That is a very significant addition, — *in*

the presence of mine enemies. We surely are
to understand by it that all around us may
stand our opponents, — pledged to do us
harm; to cut off our supplies; to starve us
out. See that ring of hostile faces, darting
fierce glances and chafing to rush upon the beleaguered soul! But they cannot cut off the
supplies that come hourly from above. They
cannot hinder the angel ministers who spread
the table and heap it up, and then form themselves into an inner ring of defence. They
may gnash their teeth at the vanity and
futility of their rage; but when God elects
to feed a soul, fed that soul shall be, though
all hell attempt to say it nay! Many a time
in David's life he ate his food in quietness
and confidence, while Saul's hostile bands
swept down the valleys and searched the
caves to find him. As it was with David, so
it has been often since.

Yes, soul, God bids thee feast: "Eat, O
beloved; yea, eat and drink abundantly."

The King doth bring thee into His banqueting-house, and His banner over thee is love. Thou shalt eat of the hidden manna, and drink of the secret spring which bubbles up in the beleaguered city, enabling it to defy the encircling lines of its foes. Nor is the time far distant when we shall sit with Christ in His kingdom; and as the far-travelled, footsore brethren of Joseph ate with the prince who once lay in the pit, so shall we sit down at the prepared table of the marriage supper, and Christ will gird Himself and come forth to serve us, and the festivities of an eternity, which shall never know penury or want, shall obliterate the memory of the sorrows of time.

IX.

"THOU ANOINTEST MY HEAD WITH OIL."

THIS similitude is borrowed from the usage of an Eastern feast, in which the welcome of the host to his guests is expressed by the precious unguents with which he anoints them on their entrance into his home. If they were as little welcome as Jesus was in the house of Simon, this act of courtesy would be omitted ; and the failure would be at once noticed, and perhaps referred to, as when the Master recalled it, saying, " My head with oil thou didst not anoint."

Love and respect could hardly manifest themselves more tenderly than by the cost-

liness of the materials which were com-
pounded to compose the oil to be lavishly
poured upon the head of the beloved guest.
Myrrh, aloes, and cassia would scent the garments with fragrance for many days, and
would be a grateful memento of happy by-
gone hours.   The lavish anointing which
Mary of Bethany shed on the head of her
Lord must have refreshed Him during the
weary hours that followed, as the delicious
scent stole up to Him from His dress, and
reminded Him of the affection of one true
heart.

These unguents, so grateful and refreshing to the scorched flesh and heated brow,
seem to have been kept in cruses of alabaster, which were easily broken, so that their
contents might be poured forth in lavish
prodigality.   How little does love reck of
cost !   When once much forgiveness has
started the flow of much love, then in the
first rapturous moments of conscious ac-

ceptance sinners will not count it waste to express their tumultuous emotions in the expenditure of the contents of precious vases, as well as in tears and kisses, and acts of tender thoughtfulness (Luke vii. 38).

When the psalmist says that God Himself anoints him with oil, does he not mean us to infer that life is a feast, in which we are guests, and God is Host? And does he also mean to teach that God greets us in love and welcome? He is not niggardly or churlish, but glad to see us glad, and to make us happy; conferring on us luxuries as well as necessaries; and taking pains, at great cost to Himself, to show us that He is well pleased to accept us, and show us grace in the Beloved.

There are many proofs of this tender grace to mankind in general. There are gleams of light in most human lives, — in the love of tender friends, or in congenial surroundings, — which speak God's welcome. To most men entering on life there is the counterpart of the Eastern oil of welcome shed on the guest entering the festal chamber. Each human life is greeted as it steps across the mystic threshold from the unseen. There is at least the mother's kiss, the elasticity of youth, the keen sense of enjoyment in natural scenes, and the absence of foreboding care.

And the blessed God has so contrived and adapted our nature to the world in which we live that there is a very ecstasy in life, and an abundance of natural joy and gladness, save where man has by sin vitiated and marred the intentions of his Creator. " How excellent is Thy loving-kindness, O God ! therefore the children of men put their trust under the shadow of Thy wings. They shall be abundantly satisfied with the fatness of Thy house ; and Thou shalt make them drink of the river of Thy pleasures." " Wine that maketh glad the heart of man,

oil to make his face to shine." "Likewise
of the fishes as much as they would."

But though this is true of men generally,
yet *there is an especial anointing* in which
they can have no part. In the Book of
Exodus (xxx. 23–25) we have a description
of a special kind of oil, " an oil of holy ointment," which was to be used to anoint the
tabernacle, and the ark, and the holy vessels, and also to consecrate Aaron and his
sons, the priests. But there were two
special provisions attached to it : first, that
it should not be imitated ; secondly, that it
should not be poured " upon man's flesh."
Each of these restrictions is worthy of note.
That it was not to be imitated surely teaches
that it sets forth some special holy unguent
in the divine chemistry which has no counterpart in human experience. And when we
further search into the sacred text, we find
that, throughout Scripture, oil is the symbol
of the blessed Holy Spirit. And we are

justified by many passages in reading this thought into the glad exclamation of the psalmist. Oh, that we might realise more constantly that our gracious Host, at whose table we sit, is constantly engaged in anointing us with the oil of the Holy Spirit!

These words with deepest significance might have been appropriated by our blessed Lord. "Unto the Son He saith, God, even Thy God, hath anointed Thee with the oil of gladness above Thy fellows." And the Apostle Peter, in the house of Cornelius, distinctly asserted such an anointing to have been communicated by the Father to the Son. "God anointed Jesus of Nazareth with the Holy Ghost and with power." And with this the united voice of the persecuted but jubilant Church accords, when it rises around the person of "Thy holy child Jesus, whom Thou hast anointed." Yes, and the Father did not give the Spirit by measure, but in unstinted abundance; the heavens were opened, — as in after-days the cruses of alabaster were broken, — and the Holy Ghost descended (Luke iii. 22).

There never was a time when Jesus was not filled with the Holy Ghost. But who can read the Scriptures attentively and thoughtfully without discovering that the anointing of the Lord Jesus at the waters of baptism endued Him with special ministerial qualifications? "The Spirit of the Lord is upon me, because He hath anointed me." "I cast out devils by the Spirit of God."

Our Lord was anointed as priest. Every priest must be anointed with the sacred oil (Exod. xxix. 21), and our High Priest, though not after the order of Aaron, must not be without so sacred a designation to His office; and thus the blessed Spirit descended and abode on Him, "like the precious ointment upon the head, that ran down upon the beard, even Aaron's beard:

that went down to the skirts of his garments." We are but as the skirts of His garments, near His feet, where the pomegranates glisten amid the tinkle of the golden bells (Exod. xxviii. 33). Yet may we not claim and expect that, as the skirts of His robes, we shall receive the sacred chrism?

Our Lord was anointed as king. "Messiah" means Anointed. "We have found the Messiah (which is, the Anointed)." And in that magnificent Messianic psalm, in which, amid the rage of His foes, the Almighty designates His Son to be the true King of men, it is distinctly stated, "Yet have I anointed my King upon my holy hill of Zion." Is there not in these glowing words a resemblance to the scene when, into the midst of the merrymaking of Adonijah and his fellow conspirators, by the stone of Zoheleth, which is by Enrogel, there broke a breathless messenger with the tidings, "Verily our lord King David hath made Solomon king. And Zadok the priest and Nathan the prophet have anointed him king in Gihon : and they are come up from thence rejoicing, so that the city rang again?" " Halleluiah : for the Lord God omnipotent reigneth." The Man of Love is God's anointed Sovereign, and though we see not yet all things put under Him, they shall be, and the world shall come to respect the power of God's irrevocable decrees.

We, too, are anointed priests and kings. Blood and oil were, as we have seen, used in the act of consecration. Our Lord, therefore, having purchased us and washed us in His blood, hath anointed us to be kings and priests unto God and His Father by the renewing of the Holy Ghost, "which He shed on us abundantly." Hast thou experienced it, my reader ? Or is this the bitter lack of thy life ? Ah, there is no favouritism or partiality with our God! That anointing is thine in the mind and intention of God; it is for thee to seek it, to appropriate it, and to allow it to be the one blessed consciousness of thy life; so that thou mayst be able to adopt the apostle's unhesitating assurance: "He which stablisheth us with you in Christ, and hath anointed us, is God; who hath also sealed us, and given the earnest of the Spirit in our hearts."

Let us never attempt to perform the work of priests in offering the sacrifice of praise or prayer or devotion without having sought for and obtained a fresh anointing. And let us be sure that it will be impossible for us to exercise any kingly function, — ruling over our inner nature, or sitting in conscious royalty with Christ on His throne, — unless we are perpetually conscious of the anointing grace of the blessed Holy Spirit.

*It is our privilege to be anointed with fresh
oil* (Ps. xcii. 10). Such was the glad assurance of the man after God's own heart.
There is nothing stale in God's household
economy. We do not need to live on dried
fruits because winter has stripped the trees.
The power and joy of other days should
be no subject for lingering regret; for our
gracious Host is able and willing to do as
much for us, and more also, on each succeeding day of our life as in any day of the past.
Sigh not for the grace of a day that is fled as
if it will never come back. There are eternal
stores and reservoirs of golden oil in God's
olive-trees, which shall pour down the golden
pipes of faith, ministering nutriment to the
lamp of holy living; so that it shall not flicker
throughout the long night, but even grow in
brilliance and radiating glory (Zech. iv. 12).
Claim each morning to be anew anointed, —
and with fresh oil.

These anointings will make us glad. It is

"the oil of gladness." "How great is His goodness, and how great is His beauty! corn shall make the young men cheerful, and new wine the maids." "Oil to make the face to shine." "Let Asher be blessed, and let him dip his foot in oil." The need of the world is — shining faces ; glad smiles ; hopeful words ; cheering toilers through the night ; and feet elastic with joy, as if bathed in its very fullness. To be without these is to miss the seal of sonship, which shall most surely authenticate it before the eyes of all men, and to become a standing libel on the gospel of Christ. But if only we acquire them, — as we most certainly shall when we are daily anointed by the Holy Ghost, — our fellows will be attracted by something in our demeanour or looks which they cannot emulate or understand ; and they will ask us to tell them the secret of a joy which the world cannot touch because its springs are hidden in a land where winter's frost is unknown.

These anointings will teach us as no human teacher could. "Ye need not that any man teach you," wrote the beloved disciple to his little children : "but the same anointing teacheth you of all things." Fret and impatience are often connected with the attainment of earthly learning from the lips of human instructors ; and often we miss the things we would most like to know. But there is nothing like this with our God. All His children are conscious that when He teaches them their peace is great. No one instructs as He does. And when He undertakes the tuition of the soul, there is no item in all the sacred lore of heavenly divinity which is omitted.

The effect of these anointings will be abiding. "The anointing which ye received of Him abideth in you." Food which we have eaten abides in us, and when we are quite unconscious of its presence it is doing its work in building up the fabric of our being. In some such way it must happen that the effect of a mighty spiritual blessing does not pass away with the moment of its first advent to the soul ; but it abides.   And amid the pressure of daily circumstance and toil and engagement, when the mind seems too set on its necessary work to have leisure for upward springing, then the Spirit will pursue His chosen office of ministering grace and strength within.   In other words, we receive benefit from the anointing of the Holy Ghost long after the immediate moment of receiving it ; the fragrance still clings about our garments, the mollifying softness still lingers on our face.

Let us never rest satisfied with anything less than that indefinable and sacred grace called "unction."   We cannot analyse it or understand why it effects what learning and eloquence fail to accomplish.   But we detect it when it is present, we miss it when absent.

With this the slightest words strike home

to the hearers' hearts as the message of God. Without it the most eloquent sentences are like unfeathered arrows, which fall useless at the archer's feet. Withhold what Thou wilt, O God, but give us the unction — *i. e.*, the anointing — of the Holy Spirit! "Thou anointest my head with oil." "Lord, not my head only, but also my hands and my feet!"

X.

THE OVERFLOWING CUP.

" My cup runneth over."

GLAD and festal moments come to the saddest and most weary hearts. At the close of a prolonged strain of anxiety, when lying exhausted on the desert sand, sleep casts its spell over the tired nature; angels spread the refreshing banquet; and the soul awakes beneath the celestial touch, invigorated for new toils.

We cannot always tell whence such experiences come; this is all we know: that the step is more elastic, the heart swells with buoyant hope, songs break from the lips, and the whole being thrills, as nature does on some lovely day of spring. "When the Lord turns again our captivity, the mouth is filled with laughter, and the tongue with singing : then we say among the heathen, The Lord hath done great things for us ; whereof we are glad."

At such hours life seems to us like a chalice mixed by the loving hand of God, and overflowing with His mercy and loving-kindness. And with tears struggling with smiles for the mastery, as rain and sunbeams on an April day, we lift the brimming cup to our lips and cry, "My cup runneth over."

A similar experience is unfolded in another psalm, which, like so many of its character, touches the lowest depths and springs, as well as the topmost heights of human experience. It begins with the plaintive notes of trouble, "the sorrows of death, and the pains of hell," and with rash imputations upon the truth of all men. It tells how in his need the psalmist called upon the name of the

Lord. It recounts the glorious deliverance there was wrought on his behalf. And now, as he reviews his lot, it seems like a cup full of salvation, charged with the prompt, gentle, and sufficient deliverance wrought for him by the Almighty (Ps. cxvi. 12, 13).

We have nothing to say now about the texture of life's cups. They may be of gold or silver or tin or alabaster or glass. There is an infinite variety in the raw material of which our lives are made. We have to deal only with ingredients, which will taste as sweet from the earthen mug as from the golden goblet. And, after all, the great differences that come to men's lives are much more in their contents than in their outward seeming. Cease looking disconsolately on the outside of thy cup and platter, but look thankfully on the contents, which may be sweeter and richer for thee, albeit that they are held in a cup of common texture, than are the contents of other lives which thou dost envy, not knowing how bitter is the draught contained within.

It becomes us to remember that "the cup of blessing" of which we drink was once filled with a bitter curse. We read in Scripture of the cup of trembling and of the cup of God's wrath ; and as we read the words we know that our lives might well have been filled with trembling and with wrath, as the just reward of our deeds ; not that God is vindictive, or that He rejoices in the death of the sinner ; but that His holy nature cannot but be roused into antagonism whenever He comes into contact with evil and impurity. If we had been left to drink the bitter results of our sin, it would have been as when Moses ground the calf to powder and strewed it upon the waters, and made the people drink. And if it be asked how it is that we have escaped so bitter an experience, the answer is given in His words who has pleaded the cause of His people : " Behold, I have taken out of thine hand the cup of trembling, even the dregs of the cup of my fury; thou shalt no more drink it again." And when He took it out of our hands, He poured its contents into the cup mixed for Himself, returning it to us emptied even to the dregs; nay, better, filled with the wine of His love and life; while He drank our potion of wrath and woe.

Remember His own words in the garden, when His agony had passed and the ruffian band was about to bind Him, and Peter impetuously and characteristically drew his sword: "Then said Jesus unto Peter, Put up thy sword into the sheath: the cup which my Father hath given me, shall I not drink it?"

Consider the ingredients of Christ's cup, — the shame and spitting; the pain and anguish; the physical torture; and, above all, the bitterness of our sins, which were made to meet in Him; the guilt of our

curse, which He voluntarily assumed; the
equivalent of our punishment, which was
imputed to Him. If we may so put it,
the human race stood in one long line, each
with a cup of hemlock in his hand; and
Christ passed along, took from each his
cup and poured its contents into the vast
beaker which He carried; so that on the
cross He "tasted death for every man."
Thus our lives brim with salvation, because
His brimmed with condemnation. Our cup
is one of joy, because His cup was one of
sorrow. Our cup is one of blessedness, because His was one of God-forsakenness.

Oh, that we might in our moments of
gladness imitate the blessed in heaven, who,
amid their greatest joys, ever associate their
happiness with the death of Christ! Never
forget the cost at which your brightest moments have been made possible.

LET US ENUMERATE SOME OF THE INGREDI-
ENTS OF OUR LIFE-CUP.

1. *Good health* is one of the chief. A
man might have everything calculated to
promote human happiness, but if all were
tinged with the pain and weariness of constant illness, what joy could he have ?   Our
sad days, when all surrounding objects are
draped in sombre hues, are, as often as not,
due to bodily weakness ; and the ecstasy of
our glad days, when sunny light lies upon
the lawn of life, is generally coincident with
a sense of vigorous health.   If, then, your
life-cup seems sweet and refreshing to your
taste, you may calculate pretty shrewdly
that good health is a main ingredient ; though
we can form no estimate of its importance
until it is withdrawn.

2. Then there are *human friendships and
affections*, the absence of which makes the
greatest prosperity a dreary desert, so that

even golden streets blister and weary the feet as if they were arid sands; but whose presence will gladden the meanest lot, so that even a garden of herbs will gleam with the glow of heaven.

3. There are also the *comforts of home life*, to say nothing of the necessaries. What a rich admixture of these do most of us enjoy! Soft pillows, carpeted floors, warm, weather-tight rooms, likewise furniture rich and plentiful; and variety of food, sufficient and comely garments, attendants who save us from harder and rougher toil. The Stoic may discipline himself to do without many of these things, and may even try to convince us that life is easier without than with them; but, nevertheless, it is undeniable that much of the enjoyment of our daily lives arises from the presence of these amenities to which we have become habituated by long custom and use.

4. There are also the *joys of the mind.*

Each can draw up from the crypt of the past the treasure in which lies the learning of the ancient and modern world ; each can collect the thoughts of poets and philosophers flung upon the strand of time as driftweed on the beach, torn by storms from ocean depths ; each can search out and drink in the wonders and beauties of nature from the wild-flowers of the forest glade.

" And those outlying worlds of many mooned spheres ;
  And that great store of stars more thickly strown in
    yonder sky
  Than dust upon the pale leaves of the auricula."

5. Now and again there is a *dash of extra sweetness* poured into life's cup, — some special deliverance, some unlooked-for interposition, some undeserved and unusual benediction, — sent apparently for no other object than to satisfy God's passion for giving. And here I must renounce my task, — no human pencil can describe all that God

pours into the lot of our life; many of the constituents are too subtle for detection; many are too divine for comprehension; many are too numerous for computation. Besides, no life-cup is mixed in quite the same proportions. Our Father carefully studies our constitution, and then suits His preparation to our need; and since we are infinitely various in our make, there is an infinite diversity in the draughts which He sets before us on the table which He spreads.

But whatever blessing is in our cup, it is sure to run over. With Him the calf is always the fatted calf; the robe is always the best robe; the joy is unspeakable; the peace passeth understanding; the grace is so abundant that the recipient has all-sufficiency for all things, and abounds in every good work. There is no grudging in God's benevolence; He does not measure out His goodness as the apothecary counts his drops and measures his drams, slowly and exactly, drop by drop.

God's way is alway characterised by multitudinous and overflowing bounty; like that in nature, which is so profuse with beauty and life that every drop of the ocean, and every square inch of the forest glade, and every molecule of matter teems with marvels, and defies the research and investigation of man. Well may we each cry with the apostle, " I have all, and abound."

On the shore of one of the vast fresh-water lakes of America stands a humble log-built cabin occupied by a family of settlers from the old country. A little child which has been playing around all the morning, and has become tired and thirsty, goes within to ask its mother for water; and the mother, taking a cup, goes with it down to the white sands on which the mimic breakers dash with musical cadence, dips it in, and lifts it, brimming and dripping with a stream of crystal drops, to her darling's lips. That is the way in which God deals with us. He gives to all liberally, and does not upbraid. There is more in Him than we can ever need; and He gives us more than we really can use for ourselves. Let us see to it that we so hold our cups as that their overflowings may not run to waste, but may drop into other cups, the cups of those that have not so much as we have. Oh, that our paths might be like the paths of God, which, when they drop fatness, drop upon the parched pastures of the wilderness, so that the little hills are girded about with joy, and become at last covered with flocks! "They shout for joy, they also sing."

But it is especially in connection with spiritual blessing that the cup most often seems to overflow. This has been the experience of many eminent saints. In one of his seasons of rapt communion John Welch, of Scotland, cried, "O Lord, hold Thy hand; it is enough. Thy servant is a clay vessel, and can contain no more!" And John Flavel

tells us that once when he was alone on a
journey his thoughts began to swell and rise
higher and higher, till at last they became an
overwhelming flood. Such was the attitude of
his mind, such the refreshing taste of heavenly
joys, and such the full assurance of his interest therein, that he truly lost the sight and
sense of this world, and of the concerns
thereof. Many years after he called that
day one of the days of heaven, and professed
that he understood more of the life of heaven
by it than by all the books he ever read, or
sermons he ever heard about it.

Certain it is that our Lord Jesus meant us
to have a more abiding experience of such
joys. He not only came to give us life, *but
life more abundantly.* He spake unto us His
inimitable words, *that our joy might be full.*
He meant our hearts to delight themselves
with fatness, and *to be satisfied with the
favour of the Lord.* His ideal for us may be
compared to those rocky basins hollowed out

by a perpetual fall of water, and lined by an infinite variety of exquisite vegetation, into which the fullness of the river, fed from perennial springs, is ever overflowing; and from which the overflow is ever passing out in a constant stream to join the eddying currents, to fill some lesser bowl beneath, or to play some part in fertilising the multitudinous flowers and plants which stretch out eager roots to its nourishing tide. Let us not hoard what we have got. Let us freely permit our cups to run over. Far from us be the niggardliness of the miser who dares not give because he fears he will not get. Let us be prodigal and spendthrift of our wealth; for we know that it is inexhaustible, being supplied from our Father's hand; and one of the laws of His kingdom is that we receive in the precise proportion with which we give.

One last word : *be sure to take the cup of salvation.* There can be no greater slight to

a giver than to have his gifts neglected. Yet
how many cups God sets before us which we
refuse to taste! Some appear to think that
God does not mean them to be thoroughly
happy; and if they drink their cups of joy, it
must be on the sly, or with words of apology.
Some only drink half; or if they drink all
they instil some bitter ingredient of their
own, lest the draught should be too delicious.
How often we forget that God has given us
all things richly to enjoy! And when we
are sure that He has given us aught, let us
not shrink from taking the cup from His
hand. Sometimes we have not because we
are too blind to see, or too slow to take the
cups which God is preparing for us.

And as we drink, let us be sure to *call upon
the name of the Lord.* Full often, if we dare
to do so, we shall find that the bitter medi-
cine which frightens us has been suddenly
changed into the very wine of life. There is
an old legend of an ancient cup filled with

poison, and treacherously placed into the king's hand. He signed the sign of the cross, and named the name of God, and it shivered at his feet. So take the name of God as your test. Name it over the cups which allure you ere you raise them to your lips, be they friendships, schemes, plans, business. That name will either show the adder that lurks in their heart, as in the goblet of the old Egyptian feast, or it will transmute common things to sacramental use, and make ordinary cups like that which we use at the table of our Lord, when over it have been spoken those memorable words, " This do in remembrance of me."

XI.

THE CELESTIAL ESCORT.

" Surely goodness and mercy shall follow me
All the days of my life."

" ALL the days." What days may not
come? *Spring days*, when all the
world shall be full of glad young life, —
frolicking in the fields; carolling in the
skies; bursting into leaf and flower at our
feet. *Summer days*, in which the year shall
have reached its glorious prime, with golden
light and long-drawn-out evenings and balmy
nights. *Autumn days*, when the fields shall
be filled with sheaves of corn, while busy
hands tear from orchard boughs and trailing
vines and towering hot-plants the rich prod-
uce of the year. *Winter days*, in which the
foot shall tread down the crackling leaves

that carpet the forest glade; days of mist
and rain and sombre light, when we gather
round the bier of the departed glory of the
year, and lay it to the dust.

We sometimes stand, as it were, on the
brow of an overhanging hill, peering wonder-
ingly into the valley at our feet, and asking
what kind of days lie there, enveloped in the
impenetrable mists, which only part as we
advance. What lies in the course of the
years? Will the days be *golden*, lit by
heaven's warm, sunny glow? Will they be
red-letter, not only in the usual sense of the
word, but because stained with the blood
of suffering and sacrifice? Will they be
drab, attired in sombre tints, dark and sad?
Birthdays; death-days; marriage-days; anni-
versaries of a dead past, which refuses to be
forgotten; fast-days; feast-days; saint-days,
because associated with some whom we have
known and loved as the very elect of God.
Only a few short hours, — like the flash of a

revolving light seen far out at sea between
two long pauses of black darkness; or like a
diamond set in ebony, — and yet how much
of weal or woe, of bitter memory or eager
foreboding, may be crowded into one brief
space of time which we call a day!

But there never will come a day throughout all the future in which we shall not have
the two guardian angels, heavenly escorts, and
God-sent messengers, *Goodness and Mercy*,
who have been told off and commissioned to
attend the believer during all the days of his
earthly pilgrimage.

When, benumbed with cold and bewildered
with the mist which has suddenly settled
down upon his track, the traveller across the
highland moor sinks down exhausted on the
drenched herbage, what an infinite comfort
it is, through a momentary rent in the mist,
to get a glimpse of the plaided figure of a
shepherd close beside him; or to discover
two servants from the distant paternal home,

sent out to scour the hills in search of the missing one, and to bring him safely to its shelter and warmth! But it is in some such way as this that the eye of the believer may detect, in moments of weariness and solitude, the presence of those twin angels of God, GOODNESS and MERCY.

We have never seen angels like the two that came to Sodom ; nor even their effigies, like the two angelic forms which bent over the ark in the inner shrine of the holy tent. But we can imagine their pure faces, their ethereal forms, their gentle ways. But here is something better than angel help: the personified attributes of God, *His* goodness, *His* mercy ; that is, *Himself,* in all the tenderest manifestations of His love and pity towards men.

Goodness AND *Mercy.* Not goodness alone, for we are sinners needing forgiveness. Not mercy alone, for we need many things besides forgiveness. But each with the other linked.

Goodness to supply every want, mercy to forgive every sin; goodness to provide, mercy to pardon. David often links these two together, as when he says, " The Lord is good; His mercy is everlasting." What shall we say of these blessed attributes? Take *Goodness*. It is laid up in vast reservoirs in the nature of God; prepared for the poor, the food of the hungry, the lodge of the righteous, the crown of the year, the very sun of life. " Oh, taste and see that the Lord is good."

" How great is His goodness, and how great is His beauty! "

Take *Mercy*. She is the daughter of God : His delight — " *He delighteth in mercy*;" His wealth — " *He is rich in mercy;*" His throne — " *I will commune with thee from off the mercy seat.*" Who shall count the rays that sparkle from this jewel! Tender, plenteous, sure, everlasting. Truly our Lord might say, " Your Father is merciful."

And they shall *follow*. In the East the shepherd always goes in front. And our Good Shepherd never puts us forth to the work or warfare of any day without going before us. But His shepherd dogs bring up the rear. We have a rear-guard against the attack of our treacherous foes. We have two strong helpers to lift us from tier to tier of the pyramid of life, keeping us from falling backward, whispering words of comfort, and placing strong hands under our arms in circumstances of difficulty and stumbling.

In that word "follow" is it possible that there is a suggestion that we are going away from God, and that He sends His goodness and mercy after us to call us back? It may be so. If a prodigal leaves a widowed mother for the sea, she never forgets him; her prayers and tears and loving thoughts follow him; and to win him back she sends out only the tenderest yearnings of a heart almost crushed. Even so with God and His own; they may wander from Him, but He follows them, He sets Goodness and Mercy on their track. Sometimes it seems as if disaster on disaster, stroke on stroke, pursues them; but it is not really so. Things are not always as they seem. And these are but the disguises which Goodness and Mercy assume; their outer garb, protecting the delicate woollen garments which are prepared for the weary head and tired limbs of the wearied, wandering, starved, and ragged prodigal. He will not break off His kindness, nor suffer His faithfulness to fail, nor forsake the works of His hands, for "His mercy endureth for ever."

You have only to turn round, or to swoon backward, and you will find yourself caught in the arms of God's goodness and mercy, which are following you always. You may not realise that they are near; you may feel lonely and sad and desolate; it may be one of your bad days, sunless and dreary, without

a ray of comfort or a flash of hope, surrounded
by objects and forms of dread.   Yet there,
close by you, evident to God's angels, though
veiled from your faithless sight, stand the
glorious, loving, pitying forms of God's infinite goodness, which cannot fail, and His
tender mercy.   They will spread you a table
in the desert as they did for Elijah ; or they
will flash through the storm and stand beside
you, bidding you *fear not*, as they did for
Paul.

> " Though unperceived by mortal sense,
>   Faith sees them always near,
>   A Guide, a Glory, a Defence :
>   Then what have you to fear? "

And in such hopes there need be no ele-
ment of doubt.   " *Surely*," says the psalmist.
Why so sure?   Because God is God, un-
changeable and everlasting ; He cannot with-
draw what He has once given.   If we believe
not, He abideth faithful ; He cannot deny
Himself.   His gifts are without repentance.

The Giver of every good and perfect gift is also the Father of lights, with whom can be no variation, neither shadow cast by turning. And when once He has begun to follow us in goodness and mercy, we may wander from His paths and neglect His love and do despite to His Spirit, ignore the presence of His messengers, and bid them begone; and yet they will not remove. They may follow at a greater distance, but they will follow still, never satisfied till they have won us back to Himself.

Surely, because God has never failed in the past. *Surely*, because it would not become Him to take in hand and not complete. *Surely*, because He has pledged Himself by exceeding great and precious promises. *Surely*, because the united testimony of all His saints attests that He never fails or forsakes. *Surely*, because if He has set His love on us in eternity, He is not likely to forget us in time. So surely shall never a day come in our earthly pilgrimage in which God shall not be at our side in goodness and mercy.

Instead of *surely*, some commentators make it *only*. " *Only* goodness and mercy shall follow me." Just as in the Seventy-third Psalm they read, " God is good, and only good," — nothing but good, — " to Israel, even to such as are of a clean heart." It may be so ; and it is certainly a fact that God's dealings with us are never anything less than good and merciful. They may not seem so ; but it is sometimes a greater test of love to withhold than to give ; to deny than to consent ; to take away than to crowd the bosom full of overflowing benefits.

Fearful and fainting hearts, dreading the dark way alone, take heart ; gird yourselves with new courage ; lift up the hands which hang down, and confirm the feeble knees ! God knows how many days of life remain ; He knows their needs, their temptations, and

their sorrows ; and He pledges Himself that
as the day, so shall be the strength ; that the
day shall never come which shall be un-
blessed with His goodness and mercy ; and
that He Himself, in the person of the blessed
Lord, will be with us all the days, "even
unto the end of the age."

XII.

"THE HOUSE OF THE LORD FOR EVER."

THE passing of the years awakens in our hearts the cry for *permanence*. Our nature is keyed, not to the temporal, but to the eternal. And as we see the leaves falling before the autumn winds or littering the forest glade down which we walk in the short winter days, as the changes of the natural world compel us to remember the still greater ones which are ever carrying us out of the familiar world of our past into one as strange and undiscovered as the new world to which Columbus sailed, there arises up within us a passionate desire for a home which death cannot invade ; friendships which time cannot impair ; chaplets of never-withering flowers ;

and a condition of existence which is impervious to change.

This permanence for which we wait seems promised in the words with which the shepherd minstrel closes the psalm, which are simple as the words " home " and " mother," and quite as full of meaning. The course of the psalm is as full of change as life itself. Every sentence is a word-picture, painting in strong and vivid outlines some new scene in our earthly pilgrimage. But here the troubled stream, broken over many a stone, driven to and fro in many a sinuous bend, seems to fall into the great deep of the ocean, eternity, the music of whose waves, as they break on the shores of time, is always in the same sweet monotone, " *For ever.*"

No doubt the changes of our mortal life are all needed to fit us for the changeless. Time is the necessary vestibule or robing-room for eternity. Earth is the training-house for the real life which awaits us when the last lesson is learned and the school-bell rings. But all that is, and has been, and shall be, is just completing our character, adding finishing touches to our symmetry; and all shall be forgotten, as a dream of the night, when once we have entered on that eternity, which is permanent in the sense of never taking from us any of our true possessions, except to complete them; or in the same way that the seed is taken away, when from it is developed a higher and ever higher growth.

But better than the thought of permanence is the thought that heaven is a HOME, — it is "the house of the Lord," which is the nearest approach possible in the Old Testament to the words of Jesus: "In my Father's house are many mansions."

What a magic power there is in that word "home!" It will draw the wanderer from the ends of the earth. It will nerve sailor and soldier and explorer to heroic endurance.

It will melt with its dear memories the hardened criminal. It will bring a film of tears
over the eyes of the man of the world. What
will not a charwoman do or bear if only she
can keep her little home together?

> " Be it ever so humble,
>   There's no place like home."

And what is our great Christmas festival
but the festival of home? Homes which
have sprung into existence at the summons
of One who was homeless fitly celebrate their
anniversary on His natal day.

And what is it that makes the idea of
home so fond? Not the mere locality, or
the bricks and mortar; the gardens where
childhood used to hide; the furniture which
is associated with tender memories, — any of
which the sight of it will immediately educe.
No; it is not these that make home. These,
without the beloved forms which used to occupy them, would be a solitude in which the

survivor would find it impossible to remain.
We find our home where father, mother,
brothers, and sisters, the wife, and children
are; where the presence of the stranger
throws no shadow over the unrestrained
play of family life.

Now let us turn our thoughts to that
heaven of which we know comparatively
so little, except that our Good Shepherd is
gone thither; and see what light is thrown
upon it by the comparison instituted here
between it and home. It is surely home
in the sense of its happy social life. We
shall be as free in the presence of God as
children are in the presence of the father
and mother whom they tenderly love. We
shall know each other as well, and converse
with each other as freely, as we have done
with the merry throng of bright young
hearts with whom we have sauntered in the
woodlands gathering wild-flowers; or have
gathered around the blazing fire, when the

yule log crackled and the Christmas glee
was at its height.   Think of the large family
of noble children of all ages, — from the little
child of six up to the young man just beginning his professional or city life in the great
metropolis, — all gathering to spend a time
together in the ancestral hall, standing amid
its far-reaching grounds; and you will have
some faint conception of what the home-
going will be, when, amid the welcoming
shouts and songs of angel harps, the last
child reaches the Father's house, and the
whole family in heaven and earth is gathered
in the Father's house for ever and for ever.
Never again to part! Never again to go
out! Never again to break up the long,
happy, and glorious home festival!

These words may be read by lonely ones
in all parts of the world, over whom there
steals at times a strange homesickness :

> " Oh for the touch of a vanished hand,
> And the sound of a voice that is still!"

"Oh, to be little children again, and to have others providing for our comfort and our joy, instead of having to fend for ourselves, and to be the source of all to others!" And mingling with such natural back-yearnings there may be the tears of recent bereavement; the thought of graves so new that the flowers have not had time to root themselves in the fresh soil.

Come, it will not do for us to indulge thoughts like these! They unfit us for the stern realities of life. They unnerve us. Let us not dwell on them. If the paradise of the past is *lost*, so that an angel stands with drawn sword forbidding our return, there is another and a better paradise before us, at whose gates beckoning angels stand, — the paradise of our Father's home. Let us not think of separation, but of reunion. In olden days the crews of outgoing vessels, till they reached the line, used to toast *Friends behind;* but as soon as they had passed it, they began to toast *Friends before*. Let us set our thoughts on the friends before us, who, thank God, are those whom "we have loved long since and lost awhile."

Blessed are the homesick, for they shall reach home.

There is great certainty in these words. The psalmist has no doubt that he will be there. Yet he had been a wandering sheep; his record by no means stainless; his temper rather that of a man of war and blood than that of peace and gentleness and love, which would befit the meek denizen of heaven. How should he come there? And what made him so sure? He doubtless felt that the Good Shepherd could not be there while the sheep was bleating piteously without. "Where I am, there ye shall be also." And we have a yet more sure word of promise to which we may joyfully take heed as to a light which shines in a dark place.

Because we have trusted Christ and are one with Him; because we have received into our hearts the germ of eternal life, which carries with it heaven in embryo; because we have the earnest of our inheritance already in the presence and witness of the Holy Ghost; because God's promise and oath assure us of our eternal blessedness, two things which make disappointment impossible, — for all these reasons and others the humblest, most timid, and weakest believer that reads these lines may dare affirm, "I will dwell in the house of the Lord for ever."

There seems to have been a sense in which David enjoyed heaven before he got there. To him the Lord's house was not simply a thing in the future, but a possibility for the present. In another psalm he talks of dwelling in the secret place of the Most High, and in yet another he employs the noble words, "One thing have I desired of the

Lord, that will I seek after; that I may dwell in the house of the Lord all the days of my life, to behold the beauty of the Lord, and to inquire in His temple." The French version of Dr. Segond is so beautiful that I am compelled to quote it also : " *Je demande à l'Eternel une chose, que je desire ardemment. Je voudrais habiter toute ma vie dans la maison de l'Eternel, pour contempler la magnificence de l'Eternel et pour admirer son temple* " (Ps. xxvii. 4). But this man was full of royal business ; he could not literally dwell in the sacred courts, for which he pined more than hart ever panted for water brooks, or doves for their cotes.

Yet can we doubt that his fervent prayer was answered, and that the fixed purpose of his heart reached its ideal ? There was, no doubt, a sense in which, whether at home in the palace of Mount Zion, or away in the desolate wastes beyond Jordan, he did dwell in the house of the Lord, beholding His beauty and inquiring His will. What is the house of God but the presence of God, habitually recognised by the loving and believing spirit ; all-encompassing, all-enveloping, all-pervasive, like the genial atmosphere of spring?

Why should not we also begin to live in the house of God, in this hallowed and blessed sense? Our heaven may thus date, not from the moment in which we first " enter the gates of the city," but from that in which we first wash our robes and make them white in the blood of the Lamb. Always and everywhere we may find our dwelling-place in God, who has been the home and refuge and abiding-place of His people in all generations. Always and everywhere we may retreat into Him from the windy storm and tempest. Always and everywhere we may make His nature not only our fortress and strong tower, but our oratory, our temple. May the Holy Spirit make real to each of us this possibility

of living in the house of the Lord hourly
and daily ; where all tears are wiped as soon
as shed ; whither cares cannot invade ; and
where the Good Shepherd leads His flocks
ever into green pastures, so that they cannot
hunger ; and beside still waters, so that they
cannot thirst ; and in cool, deep glens, so that
the sun cannot smite by day, nor the moon
by night !   Heaven before we reach heaven !

*Let us see to it that we live on this heavenly
level.*   There are many possible levels on
which we may elect to live.   That, for instance, of the church to which we belong, or
the Christian society in which we mix.   The
conventional level of doing what others do,
and being content with an average mediocrity.
This, however, ill becomes those who follow
on to apprehend that for which Jesus Christ
once apprehended them.

But there are two other levels which especially claim our thought, and between
which we must make our choice: there is

the level of our standing in Jesus Christ, and there is the level of our experience or emotional life. According to the first we have already passed through death to the resurrection and ascension side, and are already seated in the golden light which beats around the throne of Jesus. According to the other, which fluctuates with every atmospheric or physical change, we are now lifted on the crest of the billow into the sunny air, and anon flung, weary and broken, on the sand, from which the waves have ebbed, leaving us beyond their reach.

The one is the level on which God means us to live. The other is that which we have selected for ourselves, — and a sorry change it is! What wonder that we are so disappointed and disheartened! We have put the bitter for the sweet; the temporal for the eternal; the fluctuating and transient for God's unmoved and unmovable found tion, which is changeless as His love.

It is a serious question for each one to ask, "What is the level of my life? Is it mine, or my neighbour's, or God's? Am I living as a risen and ascended one, behind whom is sin and death, while above is the uncreated light of eternity?" Alas! so many of us are levelling our appreciation of our standing down to the lowness of our experience, instead of seeking to level our experience and practice up to the height of our standing in Jesus!

Now faith, when in proper exercise, does two things. First, it reckons that a position belongs to it which we do not feel, but which it dares to claim on the warrant of God's Word. Second, it lays hold on the power of God to make that position a reality in daily and hourly experience.

We do not always feel that we are where the burning words of the apostle declare us to be. In Romans vi., Ephesians ii., and Colossians iii., he affirms that we are risen and enthroned, regnant with Jesus, while His foes and ours are beneath our feet. But faith lays hold of these clear teachings of the Word of God and dares to call feeling a liar, while it holds God's Word as truth. Yea, and faith goes further. Constantly it lays hold on the almighty power of God, the power that raised Jesus from the grave of Joseph to set Him at the right hand of the Majesty in the heavens. And in the might of that power it walks across the unstable wave and climbs the steeps of air, and holds its own, its position as on the throne, against all the assaults of hell. It is impossible to live the ascension or heavenly life, which is certainly ours, without ascension and divine power. But that is within the reach of an appropriating faith (Eph. i. 19).

It is very needful for us to invoke the aid of the Holy Spirit to maintain us ever in this attitude of surrender and faith, drawing down into our lives God's constant grace. He is the Spirit of memory, who preserves us in a continual state of recollection, and who prompts us at the hour of temptation, "bringing all things to our remembrance."

And if only we live thus, life will pass on happily and usefully.   Its stay will shape itself into a psalm, like that which David, the shepherd and king, sang centuries ago.   It may begin with the tale of the shepherd's care for a lost and truant sheep.   But it will not stay ever on that level ; it will mount and soar and sing near heaven's gate ; it will spend its days on the level of those shining table-lands where God Himself is Sun ; and it will finally pass into that holy and glorious home circle, each inhabitant of which may affirm, without the least shadow of presumption or of fear, " I will dwell in the house of the Lord for ever."

THE END.